MICRONESIAN CUSTOMS
AND
BELIEFS

D1554299

This book is dedicated to
Those who lived it and wrote it,
And to those who read it.

Some Things of Value . . .

MICRONESIAN CUSTOMS AND BELIEFS

REVISED EDITION

by The Students of
The Community College of Micronesia

Compiled and Edited
by
Gene Ashby

Rainy Day Press
Eugene, Oregon and Kolonia, Pohnpei

First Edition Published in 1975 by
The Education Department,
Trust Territory of the Pacific Islands,
Saipan, Mariana Islands, 96950.

Second Printing in 1983 by
Rainy Day Press,
Eugene, Oregon 97403

Library of Congress Catalogue Number
82-060520

International Standard Book Number
0-931742-12-9

Published by Rainy Day Press
Box 3035   (and)   Box 574, Kolonia
Eugene, Oregon 97403   Pohnpei, F.S.M., 96941

Printed in USA

Acknowledgments

The students and former students of the Community College of Micronesia who lived and wrote *Some Things of Value* certainly deserve the most credit for this anthology.

The first edition of Micronesian customs was published by the Education Department, Trust Territory of the Pacific Islands, the late Mr. David Ramauri, Director. The second printing of the book was made possible by Governor Resio S. Moses of Pohnpei State (then president of the Community College of Micronesia). Their encouragement is sincerely appreciated.

For this revised edition, special thanks are extended to Ms. Iris Falcam, Librarian of CCM, for her support and proofreading of the manuscript. The maps used have been redrawn by the editor from a number of sources, but primarily: *Maps of Micronesia*, Lands and Survey Division, Trust Territory of the Pacific Islands, Saipan, 1973; *Maps of the Islands of Micronesia*, Research Section, U.S. Commercial Company Economic Survey, 1946; and *Guide to Place Names* in the Trust Territory of the Pacific Islands, compiled by E.H. Bryant Jr., Honolulu, 1971. The illustrations of Micronesian objects and scenes were drawn by James Yorlang (Yap) and Wilson Johannes (Palau), former CCM students. Six of the stories in the chapter about traditional legends and beliefs previously appeared in *Never and Always*, another CCM publication.

As usual, Mike Helm, publisher of Rainy Day Press, helped with advice and suggestions. Thanks are also extended to Dennis Hunt, Editing & Design Services, Eugene, Oregon, for assisting with the layout of this edition.

Student Writers

Yushiro Albert
Yunis Anson
Albert Augustine
Simon Awi
Kohber Biza
Fatima Carlos
Richard Carlos
Timotje Clement
Bahmer Daniel
Tridell Elidok
Julita Elnei
Rasauo Fine
Tony Finiiray
Remikio Frank
Akiro Fred
Alanso Fred
Helbert Fritz
Nesihna George
Ben Graham
Severina Gurwag
Thomas Hapitmai
Florensio Harper
Antreas Hedgar
Yalmer Helenberger
Marihne Henry
Mark Henry
Taitos Hikarip
Altred Hitchfield
Abram Ichin
Augustin Igeral
Spedin James
Ignathio Rakilur
Josua Ruben
Ermick Rudolph
Nihlo Samuel
Dismis Sandei
Suda Sefich
Vicente Seman
Heteo Shrew
Judah Sigrah
Salvino Soaladaob
Cynthia Taitano
Dorothy Tenorio
Connie Theodore

Spedin James
Paul Jibke
Akiosy John
Ben Jorkan
Bedinin Joseph
Hackney Kahn
Krispin Kaspar
Moleince Kephas
Elizabeth Kintoki
Esetong Kimiuo
Kuniuo Kiris
Ygnasia Lahasudep
Guada Lawegmay
Evelyn Lebehn
Arthur Lewis
Susan Ligow
William Macaranas
Peter Mangiemar
Hiram Malolo
Bermihna Martin
Deruit Maruame
Keep Maruame
Mercedes Megreos
Kathy Bathery
Carman Ngirmidol
Moses Noda
Goodyear Panuel
Jefferson Peter
William Radolfetheg
Philip Raiguami
Leo Thineyog
Moses Thomas
Peter Tigiwyar
Albert Tilfas
Michuo Timothy
Joe Tiucheimal
Johannes Tsuneo
Weldis Welley
Alexander Willy
Maria Yamada
Vincent Yangremal
Norbert Yiftheg
Stan Yiluy

Preface

The islands of Micronesia have undergone considerable political adjustments resulting from plebicites six years ago. The former districts of the U.S. Trust Territory of the Pacific Islands have been divided into the Republic of Belau (formerly Palau District), the Commonwealth of the Northern Mariana Islands (formerly Mariana Islands District), the Federated States of Micronesia (formerly Yap, Truk, Ponape, and Kosrae Districts), and the Republic of the Marshall Islands (formerly Marshall Islands District). Political division, however, does not necessarily include cultural estrangement, and so the customs practiced on a number of islands remain similar, despite linguistic and political differences —and separation by thousands of miles of the Western Pacific.

If a visitor only comes to the population centers of the area, the unique aspects of Micronesian culture are hardly evident. Some centers resemble the American frontier more than the Pacific island paradise of tourist brochure fame. Beyond these centers, however, and in direct proportion to the distance away from them, traditional culture still thrives in the islands, touched only, perhaps, by the monthly visit of a "fieldtrip" vessel —and often not at all.

A well-dressed, western educated Micronesian, working in a government office, lunching at an oriental restaurant, and drinking "sundowners" at an American-style bar, might well appear on the surface to have switched cultures and adopted bastardized customs. However, this same individual can often speak three different languages interchangeably in conversation with a friend, and can move into traditional culture as quickly and completely as he can change clothes into a "thu" or a "lava lava." and with a truly remarkable ability to fit comfortably in both.

The writers of these chapters were wearing one set of clothes while writing about another. They are all former students of the Community College of Micronesia, and were not trained researchers when they wrote about their customs. But even in a western orientated classroom using the English language, many aspects of their "Micronesian personality" refused to desert them. They asked that their names not appear on their individual papers —"It should be the elders that get credit for telling about traditional culture. . ." Whether Marshallese or Palauan, Chamorro, Yapese or Kosraean, their attitude seems to have been summed up by William R. Bascom when he wrote about Pohnpeians:

> A deep sense of pride that cannot be expressed openly, a hunger for praise and recognition when it is deserved, a retiring modesty, tolerence and patience, together with quiet dignity are characteristics of the . . . personality.

Gene Ashby
Pohnpei, F.S.M.

Table of Contents

REPUBLIC OF THE MARSHALL ISLANDS

MAPS AND ILLUSTRATIONS

ILLUSTRATIONS

INTRODUCTION TO THE REVISED EDITION

"Micronesia" was formerly a cultural designation —the word is taken from the Greek "mikros" meaning small, and "nesos" meaning island— along with Polynesia to the east and Melanesia to the south. The area, however, contains eight different languages and enough dissimilar ethnic groups so that a cultural designation is no longer sufficient. At present, Micronesia is considered to be a geographical area in the Western Pacific Ocean, approximately three million square miles of sea and seven hundred square miles of dry land—an inhabitable area about half the size of the smallest U.S. state, Rhode Island. (The island of Guam, a U.S. territorial possession in Micronesia is not included in these chapters.)

The 175,000 people of the former U.S. Trust Territory of the Pacific Islands live in four newly created political entities. From west to east they are Republic of Belau (16,000 people), the Commonwealth of the Northern Mariana Islands (45,000 people), the Federated States of Micronesia (110,000 people), and the Republic of the Marshall Islands (40,000 people). Some 2,200 islands and islets are sprinkled on a wavy line the length of the continental United States from east to west. About one hundred of these specks of land are regularly inhabited.

The customs of Micronesians are similar in generalities from Palau to the Marshalls, but vary considerably in particulars. Those described in the following chapters relate to: childbirth; land and food; marriage; traditional legends and beliefs; the practice of skills; and funerals. Islands and atolls containing all but about five percent of the people are represented in this book, and in most instances it is the first published writing by Micronesians about customs on their own islands. The sections are arranged by political entities, geographically from west to east. Topics begin with childbirth and are followed by land and food, marriage, legends and beliefs, skills, and funerals. Information on all of these topics is included for the larger islands such as the Palaus, Yap, Truk, Pohnpei, and Kosrae.

To this revised edition have been added superstitions and beliefs. Some are particular to specific islands or groups, and others are known throughout Micronesia. (Sweeping a floor at night will bring bad luck from Koror to Majuro.) Some beliefs mentioned are taken from local proverbs. It was the original intention to write the proverbs in vernacular languages and then translate them directly into English. As it turned out, however, the translations are hardly self-explanatory. "*Tikin wol*" in Pohnpeian literally translated means "Smallness of a man," for instance. The actual meaning of the proverb is that even though a man is not impressive in size, he can still be the equal of any other man. It is also a warning to behave with proper modesty and deference around all men, regardless of their size. The popular Pohnpeian proverb "*Nennenin sarau kommwoad*" literally translated means "Quietness of barracuda fierceness." The meaning, however, is that a man should be silent, unobtrusive, and inconspicuous, but should strike violently when necessary. Consequently, the beliefs communicated in proverbs are given, rather than a direct translation.

The sea dominates island life and is so ever-present that it also permeates proverbs, sayings, and superstitions, and beliefs. Fish are very frequently used to illustrate a non-marine truth— "Don't chase after an escaped fish," or don't cry over spilled milk. Rules about fishing are also wrapped in superstitions throughout Micronesia. A Chamorro fisherman off of Saipan would no more point fingers at a flock of birds over a school of fish than would a Kosraean fisherman off of Lelu. The stuff of tropical Pacific islands — coconuts, breadfruit and taro, and reefs and canoes and tropical birds and flowers — is used repeatedly in beliefs to instruct in manners, morals, and skills.

Maps, which include physical and cultural information about the islands on which particular customs are followed, are also included in this revised edition. Lines of latitude and longitude are added for more exact locations and to determine distances. The following chapters include thirty-five maps of individual islands on which various customs are practiced. Distances are presented in statute miles. To change to nautical miles, subtract one eighth of the distance.

Capsule physical and cultural data appears on each map. Population and household figures are taken from the most recent census in Micronesia, 1980. The seven historical culture groups of Palauans, Southwest Islanders, Mariana Islanders, Yapese, Central Carolinians, Eastern Carolinians, and Marshallese are those of Douglas L. Oliver in *The Pacific Islands*. Francis X. Hezel's language group designation in *Micronesia through the Years* is used: Palauan, Trukic, Yapese, Chamorro, Pohnpeian, Kosraean, Polynesian, and Marshallese. The population center and the political affiliation of the island is also included. A belief, usually taken from a proverb known on the particular island, appears on each map.

Finally, twenty-three illustrations of aspects and objects of Micronesian culture appear in the revised edition. They were drawn by James Yorlang from Yap and Wilson Johannes from Palau, two former students of the Community College of Micronesia.

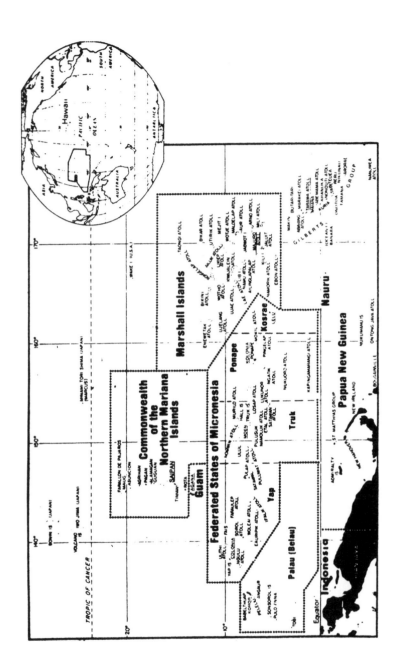

MICRONESIAN CUSTOMS
AND
BELIEFS

Childbirth

Childbirth customs on fourteen islands and atolls from Koror to Likiep are described. These islands have populations ranging from tiny Mokil with 268 to Pohnpei with 33,000.

The birth of a child is by far the most important occasion in island life, and so prenatal and postnatal care are closely controlled and supervised. Requirements for the pregnant women and expectations vary from island to island, and sound medical practices are often joined with traditional spiritualism and medicines.

During the actual delivery, all male members of the family are asked to leave the area, and only women attend to the expectant mother. During labor, she is expected to keep silent and show as little pain as possible. In recent years, a number of births have taken place in hospitals in the population centers where male doctors naturally assist in the delivery. The tradition of pride in hiding pain, however, always enters the hospital along with the expectant mother.

Following a successful birth, restrictions continue to be imposed on the new mother. Her aunts, older sisters, mother, mother-in-law, and her grandmothers always assist and provide modern and traditional medicines. The role of the husband and other male relatives is usually minimal at this time, except to provide necessary facilities, foods (especially fish), and other necessities required by the mother and child.

For the young Micronesian mother, her own first childbirth is the culmination of a learning process that began some eighteen years previously. Since then, she had had numerous experiences in child care —helping female relatives in cleaning, bathing, clothing, feeding, and keeping babies occupied. As a child, she had looked after infants —carrying them on her hip when she was hardly larger than the babies. As a teenager, she had looked after children, and as a young adult, she had supervised her younger brothers and sisters.

After the birth, one or more of four festivities or ceremonies might take place (usually all four take place). An impromptu party might be held to celebrate the birth; a feast and celebration could be held a few days later when the infant is first shown to his relatives and friends of the family; a baptism ceremony and party might take place later; and a large celebration upon the first anniverary of the birth is always held.

A number of pregnancies are unintended in Micronesia, but few are unwanted because of the important assets that children bring to a family. If the new mother is unmarried, it is frequently the grandmother of the infant who decides who will care for him. In many cases, the grandmother will raise the child as her own.

Adoption of children is common in Micronesian custom, and assures that all who want a child may have one. Unlike adoptions in the U.S., legal fees are not necessary, however. Adoption usually takes place after an oral agreement between families during the first year. They are almost always within the extended family or clan, or larger ethnic group, and a child may well grow up in one family within sight of his biological mother. Some "adoptions" are temporary or for short periods of time. A child might live with one family for some time, and then move in with another for a particular convenient reason. These changes in residence occur most often when a child must leave home for schooling. Legal adoptions by non-Micronesians are not at all common in the islands.

Children in Micronesia are born into a number of traditional social structures, of which they will soon become quite aware. They are, of course, welcome members of a nuclear family, whether the mother is married or not. They are also members of a clan through the line of the mother, and will tend to associate more with other members of the same clan when they grow up. They are also part of a political division, usually a municipality, which in many cases was a former "tribe" or kingdom, and still retains a traditional chief. All of this, in addition to being a citizen of the Republic of Belau, the Commonwealth of the Northern Mariana Islands, the Federated States of Micronesia, or the Republic of Marshall Islands.

Land and Food

Of the one hundred or so inhabited islands of Micronesia, only Babelthaup, Yap, Saipan, Tinian, Pohnpei and Kosrae are larger than seven square miles in land area—about eighty populated islands contain less than three square miles of land. The population density varies from lows of less than a hundred people per square mile on a number of isolated atolls to 16,895 people per square mile on Majuro in the Marshall Islands. For the 175,000 people of Micronesia, land is the ultimate physical possession, and especially land that can produce food.

The main locally grown staple foods are breadfruit, taro, yams, pandanis, cassava, sweet potatoes and arrowroot. Consequently, the traditional basic item in the Micronesian diet is a starchy fruit or vegetable, and is usually accompanied by a protein dish of seafood, chicken or meat.

The crops that are cultivated in the islands are fairly easy to tend, but all have limitations on their availability. Breadfruit, for instance, is seasonal, although there is an early and a late bearing variety. It also grows better on the high islands than on the atolls of Micronesia. Taro grows all year around, but the cultivated variety requires fresh water in swamps. (A typhoon hitting an atoll can cause damage that will make a taro swamp brackish for years and halt cultivation completely.) Yams can be harvested all year around, but must be protected from foraging animals such as pigs. They require more attention than breadfruit or taro and grow much better on high islands than on atolls. Pandanis and cassava (tapioca) are common on both atolls and high islands, but these foods lack the nutrient value of their starchy cousins breadfruit, taro, and yams. Fruits are usually eaten at the end of meals or as between-meal snacks. The most common are bananas, mangoes, papayas, citrus, limes, mountain apples, and coconuts.

Coconut palms are the most useful trees in Micronesia, and every part of the tree has a function that Micronesians use. For growth, however, they require year-around warm temperatures, abundant moisture and sunlight, low altitudes, and soil that will allow for good drainage. When mature, each tree produces about fifty nuts per year. From the nut comes the "meat" eaten at meals or mixed with other foods. The dried meat becomes *copra*, Micronesia's largest cash crop. The liquid is used as a cool drink or in cooking, and oil is also produced from the coconut. The hard shell makes a convenient container and is also used to make charcoal. Husks are used to weave *sennet* for bindings, and are also woven into thatch, although pandanas, and ivory nut palms are preferred for thatch roofing. The thick trunks of palms are very strong and often used in heavy construction.

Fish is more frequently eaten on atolls than on high islands in Micronesia and is a main source of protein. Pigs are the most coveted meat, but dogs and poultry also supply a source of protein in the diet. Grazing animals are few because of the limited acreage, except on a few high islands and the ranches of Tinian in the Marianas.

No one goes hungry on an island of Micronesia unless the entire island is suffering from famine. When visitors arrive at a home, they are served food immediately (or served an excuse telling why none is ready or available). Other aspects of Micronesian culture may change perceptably within decades, but the spirit of sharing whatever is available, even (or especially) with strangers, is as prevalent in Micronesia today as in generations past.

Marriage

Of traditional customs in Micronesia, courting, marriages and wedding procedures have probably changed more than any others since the arrival of the Christian missionaries in the middle of the last century. Even in marriages, however, requirements and customs from the past are preserved. Actually, rituals have changed much more than conventions.

Throughout Micronesia, monogamy has always been prevalent. Only chiefs and a few other affluent individuals were allowed the luxury (or mixed blessing) of more than one wife. Even for those few who practiced polygamy, however, one wife was considered to be the "real" one and exerted a very strong influence over the household.

As in the past, unions mostly take place within the larger ethnic group of the couple. Since all societies in Micronesia are exogomous, members of the same clan never married. Consequently, a woman's husband and her children are of different clans. (All Micronesian groups are matrilineal, and so clanship is passed through the mother.) Arranged marriages, where parents or other relatives determined the partners, were quite common in the past, and they do take place at present. Land, wealth, and social rank and status were always key considerations in this type of marriage arrangement.

Premarital sex was much more accepted before the arrival of the missionaries than at present. Fidelity of married women, however, has always been expected in most Micronesian societies.

At present, premarital activities are controlled by conventions and dominated by families. These mores are similar in all Micronesian ethnic groups. Open "dating" so common in western societies, is not accepted in Micronesia, and couples are seldom seen together in public before marriage. To make contact with a young lady, the man might try through an intermediary—usually a female friend of the lady—or by sending her a note. If the lady is interested, the couple will meet secretly at night on a number of occasions until they decide to marry.

For the proposal of the marriage, prominent relatives along with the suitor's father will visit the home of the lady. (She might have told her parents of the forthcoming visit, but just as likely might not have.) After discussion, in which the possiblility of incest is a key consideration, if the proposal is accepted, the young lady might leave her home with the man's relatives, and from then on be considered married. In some groups, the man is required to live with the lady's family for a sort of trial period. In others, a formal Christian church ceremony must take place before the couple is accepted as being married.

Wedding ceremonies usually take place on weekends at a Catholic or Protestant church, and are similar to those in western societies, except that no kissing takes place. Following the ceremony, a large feast is provided by both sides of the family and gifts are presented to the newly married couple.

Traditionally, the couple resides with the family of the young man. The new wife certainly does not completely leave her relatives, but she then owes her allegiance and support to the family of her husband.

Changes in marriage customs seem to have accelerated in recent years. Divorce, either legal or de facto, has become more common than in the past. (When a second marriage takes place, traditional conventions are not nearly as restrictive as in a first marriage.) Some couples are "married" by simply living together with community acceptance, if not approval. Another recent change is an increase in marriages between Micronesians and non-Micronesians probably brought about by so many Micronesian students in higher education abroad.

Legends and Beliefs

Myths and legends in Micronesia are part of a rich heritage of oral literature. Most fall into three categories that often overlap: there are historical tales purported to be true; there are stories told for instruction or to communicate a particular moral or set of values; and there are stories told simply for amusement.

Islands have a number of similar characteristics by nature of their geography, and so do legends told about them. Consequently, similar themes in stories are known, with some variations, on islands from Palau to the Marshalls. A common theme is of land being raised from the sea or torn apart by human hands. Another is of birds, fish and animals taking on human qualities for good or for evil. In Micronesian legends, magic prevails, and scientific truths take a well-deserved holiday.

Legends illustrate beliefs of a group of people, and so do stories about important aspects of their cultures—Yapese stone money, outer island sailing rules, local leadership, *sakau* drinking, magic love perfume, clans and extended families show unique aspects of particular islands.

Micronesians have an intimacy with the sea for better or for worse—a forced marriage one might say brought about by necessity. Consequently, moods of oceans and marine life are personified in the mythology of the islanders. As mentioned earlier, marine creatures are often used to illustrate accepted morality, and catching fish is thought to be determined by adhering to traditional superstitions as much as by the skill of the fisherman.

A remarkable characteristic of Micronesians is a willingness to believe and adopt. The monster Lowakalle of Arno in the Marshalls would be readily accepted by the girl who turned into a sea cow in Palau; the love perfume of the Mortlock Islands could easily be used by the magicians of Yap.

Traditional Skills

The bare essentials of living have dominated Micronesian societies for centuries. Consequently, skills associated with these necessities have always been important in the culture. The skills of carpentry for construction of structures and canoes, and fishing and agriculture for subsistence living are practiced on all islands of Micronesia to varying degrees.

Historically, nearly every group produced a specialty that could be used as trade items after voyages to other islands. Recently, the demand by visitors coming to Micronesia has stimulated the practice of some skills that have slumbered for years—storyboard carving in Palau, decorative weaving and carving in Kapingamarangi, and creating new shell ornaments for jewelry in the Marshall Islands.

Social mobility in traditional Micronesian societies is quite restricted, and status is usually determined by birth. However, the skilled craftsman or artisan is highly respected, and receives considerable local prestige. His individual competence in a specialized skill is always in demand, and rightly so. Under the direction and supervision of a master artisan, and with the assistance of people in the community, a home or a canoe house could be built with local material in a single day.

The atolls of Micronesia are generally infertile compared to high islands such as Kosrae, Pohnpei, Yap and Babelthaup. Consequently, high islanders are more skilled in agriculture. Palauans, for instance, are known for their cultivation of taro and Pohnpeian men are famous for the skill used in growing their prized yams and sakau plants.

Skills in Micronesia have always been taught within extended families and clans, and learned in much the same manner as an apprentice would learn plumbing in the United States. Plastic and metal tools have replaced coral and shell, but the master Pohnpeian stone mason, Marshallese navigator, Kapingamarangan fisherman, and Yapese canoe builder still occupy unique and prestigious positions in MIcronesian culture—and outside of it as well.

The book has not been written about the skill of curing ailments with local medicines. The main reason is that these cures are prized information, learned from years of experience, and so information about them is not given away casually. The practicianers of these skills are both men and women, as are the expert masseurs and masseuses whose services are so frequently in demand in the islands.

The need for physical strength and skills of warfare such as throwing spears has ceased since wars between islands have ended. However, recreation skills for friendly competition have been developed in canoe paddling, swimming, and western track and field events recently. Competitions between municipalities or other island groups are now quite common, and the skilled champion once again wears the *mwaramwar*.

Funerals

"No man is an island entire onto himself," especially in Micronesia. The loss of a member of an island community is felt more poignantly by more people than in less interpersonal societies. "For whom the bell tolls..."?

On most islands in Micronesia, the tolling of a church bell with a particular cadence at an irregular time, indicates that a death has taken place. On high islands with a radio transmitter, a local broadcast spreads the sad news. Except on these islands with relatively large populations, the sad news is seldom completely unexpected unless the death occurred because of an accident. In small island communities where everyone knows everyone else's affairs, they also know each other's ages and physical conditions.

Whether spread by word of mouth or by radio, friends and relatives of the deceased flock to his home. (The body will have been prepared by women and will be displayed in the largest room.) A continual wailing is heard from women crying as they view the corpse. Men, however, try to show as little emotion as possible in public, but are not always successful. At this first funeral gathering, coffee, canned meat, bread and biscuits—foods that take little preparation—are served, and the mourning goes on throughout the night. Often a local religious choir will arrive to sing. A basket is usually placed near the body for cash contributions that will be used by the family to defray funeral expenses.

With the coming of dawn, visitors usually return to their homes to gather local foods in season, pigs, chickens, and dogs for the funeral feast that will take place following the burial.

Burial takes place on the day following the death, unless there are circumstances that delay it. (One might be waiting for the arrival of a close relative from a distant islet or atoll.) Since there are no large cemeteries in Micronesia, the burial is usually on one's land or that of a close relative.

The grave will have been prepared before the coffin is nailed shut. (The pounding of nails into the coffin signals a finality that precipitates extreme crying and wailing among female mourners.) The funeral procession then accompanies the coffin to the burial site. Following a short religious service, the coffin is lowered into the grave and buried. A few days later a concrete enclosure might be poured to border the grave, and a marker, cross, or tombstone placed at its head. It is also common to build a small shelter over the grave.

A very important occasion at a funeral is the feast that follows the burial. Families spare no expense at this time because it indicates to the community how much the family cared for the person who died. The prestigious food brought is pork, and foods are most often cooked in a traditional oven temporarily constructed of heated stones. When mourners leave the funeral feast, they are expected to take with them a large plate of food to eat later.

The immediate family of the deceased along with some close friends stay together after visitors have left. The period of active mourning varies in length. It is usually about four days, but could be as long as several months. In recent years, schooling and government employment have had an effect on the length of the mourning period for some family members.

One year after the death, a final feast is usually held. This anniversary remembrance takes place at the home of the deceased, and could be as lavish as the funeral feast. However, the solemnity of the occasion has been dissipated by time. Speeches are made extolling the virtues of the deceased and family and friends contribute food and money for the occasion.

The size of funerals in Micronesia varies, as does the number of people who attend them. The largest and most lavish funerals are held for chiefs, clergymen, and political leaders, and the smallest are held for infants. There are no mortuaries or trained undertakers in Micronesia, and so community involvement and cooperation continue to be outstanding characteristics of funerals in the islands.

There are a number of unique aspects to Micronesian funerals. Unlike those in the West, close family members of the deceased —sisters, brothers, aunts, uncles—

work the hardest at funeral activities. Perhaps this activity is beneficial to the bereaved by allowing them to temporarily take their minds off of their sorrow. Other than in the area surrounding the coffin, the mood at a funeral, although sad, is not extremely unhappy. Wailing and mourning are hard to sustain for days at a time, and funerals are not new to Micronesian mourners. They have attended them since childhood. Also, a fatalism about death seems to pervade Micronesian cultures more than in the West.

Republic of Belau

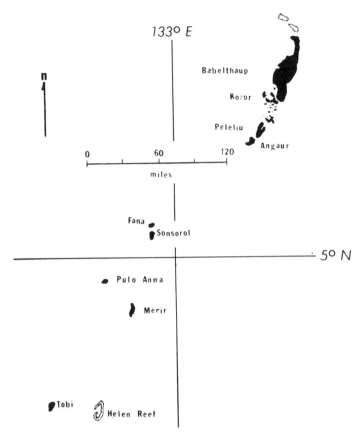

Republic of Belau

Land area: 170.43 square miles
Population: 12,172 in 2,029 households
Main Cultural Groups:
      Palauans; and Southwest Islanders
Main Languages:
      Palauan; and Carolinian (Trukic)
Population Center: Koror, Palau

You are like a bug that flies into a fire. When you see trouble, you run to it uninvited, and end up getting hurt.

From a Palauan Proverb

Palauan Meeting House, "Bai"

3

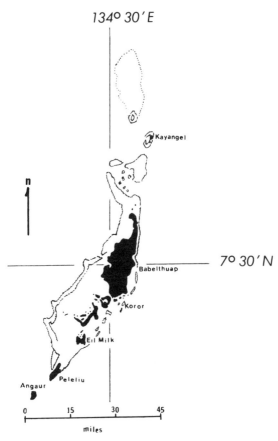

Palau Islands

Land area: 168.93 square miles
Population: 12,120 in 1,961 households
Main Cultural Group: Palauans
Main Lanugage: Palauan
Political: Republic of Belau
Population Center: Koror

Moving into a house that has not been completely built will bring bad luck to the residents.

Palauan Belief

Customs Before and After Childbirth
in Palau

When a Palauan woman becomes pregnant with her first child, traditional customs are practiced both before and after the delivery of the baby. Also, both the woman's family and her husband's family have specific responsibilities and obligations.

The responsibility of caring for an expectant mother is in the hands of her parents rather than her husband. The woman's parents appoint a member of their family, usually one of the sons, to see that she receives the best care and also that she gets the right foods and the proper amounts. At this time, she will not be permitted to walk around the community. It is believed that, if she sees someone or something unpleasant, this could affect the unborn baby.

Palauan money is important in our custom. Three months after the conception, the pregnant woman's uncle will hang one kind of money around her neck. This money is round in shape and its purpose is to assure that the head of the unborn child will develop round. The husband's uncles, aunts, and sisters who are married will also donate money that will be given to the pregnant woman's father to bring to her. The money has different purposes. Two kinds have the power to block the baby on both sides of the womb. It is believed that if the baby is allowed to sway in the womb it will be an obnoxious person when it is born. Also, money is donated to assure that the woman has no difficulties in her delivery.

After a woman has delivered her child, she will take special baths with extremely hot water. This is very important in Palauan culture. Leaves and grass that have a healing effect and a pleasant odor are added to the water. Only specialists can administer these baths as the method is not known to ordinary women, and it is the woman's mother who must find the person to give the baths. The number of days that the bath will be given depends on the rank of the woman's clan. Different clans require a different number of days. The woman's father is responsible for building a small house for the bathing and no one is permitted to enter it except the new mother and the woman who administers the baths. Special Palauan money will be given to the expert in payment for the baths. This money, "*toluk*," is made of turtle shell and is considered to be priceless.

Another treatment the woman will receive is steaming, which involves being placed over steaming water with pleasant-smelling leaves and grass in it. If the new mother is unmarried, however, the steaming water will contain no leaves and grass. It is believed that steaming helps prevent the woman from becoming dizzy in the sun.

At a ceremony held after the birth of a child, the husband's family will donate money while the wife's relatives and friends prepare food. When the husband's father and other relatives arrive, the festivities will begin. The husband's aunts will summon his wife to bring the baby into the room. When she arrives, one of the aunts will hang Palauan money around her neck. This shows to everyone, including the girl's family, that they are able to provide for the husband and wife. The money collected from the husband's family will then be given to the father of his wife. Then, an aunt will begin dancing and everyone will join in and sing for the mother and the newly born baby. Presents will be given and everyone will eat, dance, and sing until nightfall.

Palauan childbirth customs have changed little in recent times. Although many islands in Micronesia have no ceremonies or rituals before childbirth, Palauans still practice the giving of special traditional money to spiritually help the expectant mother and her unborn child. Also, the ritual of hot baths after a delivery is a custom that is particular to mothers in Palau.

If the husband of a pregnant woman goes fishing with other men, they will catch no fish.

Palauan Belief

Female Taro Farmers of Palau

In Micronesia, farming is usually done by men or shared between men and women. Therefore, it is interesting that in the islands of Palau, farming is the responsibility of the women. The cultivation of a number of crops has been influenced by foreign methods, but the cultivaton of taro remains uniquely Palauan.

It is the custom on the islands for women to cooperate and work together in farming. The land, once cleared of sticks, branches, and stumps, is prepared for planting as soon as possible. The soil is turned over by hand. The women insert their hands into the soil as deeply as possible and turn it over green fertilizer. This has been provided by young boys or other women in a family. This fertilizer is mainly the leaves of hibiscus and other trees available near the taro swamp. This stage of farming is the most difficult, and it is much harder if the soil is so soft that the women sink deeply into it. After the soil has been prepared, the water is drained from the area to facilitate planting and mulching.

After a crop of taro has been produced, the women remove the tubers and use the stalks for planting. These planting materials are inserted into a prepared patch and, at the same time, banana leaves are used to mulch the entire patch. It is believed in Palau that these leaves will help in controlling weeds from spreading. After this process, water is re-introduced after waiting about a week and one or two inches of it is maintained in the patch. This supplies the required moisture and controls weeds, rats and snails. When the plants are firmly rooted, then the water is drained to make the coming harvest easier.

The giant taro plant is much easier to grow and requires little cultivation compared to other taro. After the swamp has been cleared, the taro is simply inserted into the soil. Occasional clearing of weeds is necessary during the time that this taro is growing.

A number of other crops such as tapioca, bananas, sugarcane, sweet potatoes, and pineapples are grown and cultivated by other methods, some of which were brought to Palau by the Japanese before the American administration of the islands began. These are quite popular foods and are eaten often on the islands. Taro, however, remains unusual because it is cultivated by women and in a way that is unique to the islands of Palau.

If a hunter tells where he will hunt, or a fisherman tells where he will fish, they will have no luck in hunting and fishing.

Palauan Belief

Planting and Cultivation of Farms
in Palau

Very nearly all of the people in Palau are concentrated in the Palau Islands complex. Consequently, local customs and farming methods are much the same for most people in the area. Communal planting, woman farmers, and individual cultivation are characteristics of farming in Palau.

Women attend to the farming in Palau. Most of the food is raised by individual families, and farming is occasionally done without the help of others in the community. However, land is usually worked by a group of women from a community who come together for this purpose. The main food cultivated is taro, but other foods such as sweet potatoes, tapioca, bananas, and breadfruit are an important part of the diet.

Communal farming is initiated by a leader. When a high-ranking woman in the community sees that the families will run low on food, she calls a special meeting of all the women in her community. She makes them aware of the problem and informs them that it is time to cultivate their land. The women will work together as a group on each farm and a date will be set to begin work. At this time, it will be decided on which family's farm to start work, whose land will be second, and so on, until a schedule of work has been determined for the whole community. By our custom, all women will be required to work and to cooperate with each other until the planting has been completed. If a woman does not work without substantial reason, such as pregnancy, she will be severely criticized by the community.

When all of the planting has been completed, each individual is responsible for the upkeep of her land. The crop that is harvested will not be shared, but will become the property of each family. However, there are exceptions to this and a special occasion may arise where food is shared. The high-ranking woman in the community may request the other women to donate a certain amount of food for a particular purpose and all of the women will comply.

It is unusual in Palau for each family to live on their own farmland. In our islands, a "community" is actually an area of about fifty square miles. Women have other things to do, such as caring for children and taking care of the home. Consequently, it is difficult for them to plant alone and it is easier done working with a group of women in the community.

Taro remains the most important food in Palau, although by no means the only one. Fish is eaten often and it is the responsibility of men to catch them. At our feasts, one would also find pigs and chickens to be common.

Methods of growing most crops are much the same as on other islands in Micronesia. Probably the most outstanding features of Palauan farming are the role of men and women in the work and the way in Palauan women work together.

The coconut that contains no milk is not known until it is opened.

From a Palauan Proverb

Activities and Responsibilities
in Marriage on Palau

In Palauan custom, a man wishing to marry must depend on relatives to help him get his permission from the girl's parents. If this is received, the couple will live together for a trial period. Finally, if the trial is successful, a wedding and feast will take place.

It is, of course, necessary for a man to discuss his wishes with the girl he wants to marry. If she agrees, then both the man and the girl will have to talk to their parents about the proposal. If either set of parents is not in favor of the marriage, then the man will not be able to marry the girl he likes best. The man's parents will want a girl who has a lot of Palauan money, and this is a consideration. If both sets of parents agree, then the man has certain traditional responsibilities.

First, the man wishing to marry must ask a cousin, his father, or another important relative to accompany him to the girl's home. The reason for this is that elders are very respected in our custom. When the relative and the man enter the house, they will both sit close to the door with the suitor sitting to the left of the one who accompanies him. When the girl's parents see this, it is an indication that the purpose of the visit is to discuss marriage. If the discussion is concluded successfully, the relative will then leave and the man will remain at the home of his future bride.

After a month or two, the parents of the girl will prepare food, and this will be sent with the couple to the home of the man. Before this the parents of the man will be notified so that they can call their family together. When the food is accepted, the marriage ceremony is agreed upon.

For the wedding ceremony, friends and all members of both the families will gather together. At this time there is no singing or dancing. People will just sit and talk while the man's parents and real sisters are giving Palauan money to the bride's parents. In paying this money, it shows to all people that the couple is really married.

For the marriage feast, the bride's relatives will prepare a large amount of food and will slaughter a hog for the groom's relatives. Also at this time, the relatives of the groom will collect money and present it to the bride's relatives. The Palauan way of celebrating marriage is similar to a farewell party; after the marriage, the young woman will no longer be a part of her family and will live with her husband at his home. The food from the bride's relatves and the money from the groom's should always equal each other in value. Also, at wedding feasts, clan status is a consideration.

Following the marriage, the couple usually stays at the home of the husband or with his parents if he does not have a house of his own. Although living apart from her family, the woman still has certain obligations to them for which her husband is responsible. In Palauan custom, the man is the financial sponsor for his wife. He must contribute money for his wife when her male relatives buy their homes. He must also provide money for his father-in-law whenever he engages in Palauan business customs. The wife must contribute food when a relative of hers dies, and this donation is the husband's responsibility. Money for dowries is expected when the wife's relatives get married, and her husband must provide this.

Divorce during the past several decades has usually been initiated by the husband's relatives. It is very important in Palau for a woman to cooperate. If the relatives of a man feel that his wife is not participating in their business customs or helping other relatives, they will tell the husband to divorce his wife. The American system of individual families has had an effect on Palauan customs. Now, some couples simply take care of their own affairs without considering traditional family responsibilities.

Sneezing repeatedly means that someone is thinking of you.
Palauan Belief

How the Islands of Palau Were Formed

The Palau Islands are separated by numerous channels and lagoons, but long ago, the islands are believed to have been one large land mass. How the land was broken into islands, and why people have different characteristics on the islands, is a story often told in Palau.

Today, the island of Angaur sits some five miles across the sea from its neighbor, Peleliu. It is believed, however, that Angaur and Peleliu were once a single piece of land. On the area of land there lived a very unusual man named Uab.

When Uab was only a child he would not play with other children, but was content to eat large amounts of food and to sleep. Even when he was very young he would eat much more food than adults, and so he grew to be enormous. As he got older, he ate more and more. Soon he was eating all of the food that his family could produce, and then he consumed all of the food of his neighbors as well. And he continued to grow larger and larger. Uab even had to move out of his house because it became too small for his huge body. Day by day, week by week, and year by year, Uab continued to grow. Finally, he was eating all of the food in the community and people were starving, just to feed the ever-hungry Uab.

Uab's neighbors had to do something or they would all soon starve to death. They all met together and decided to burn the gigantic Uab and end their misery. So they built a large fire in a circle around the unsuspecting giant.

The fire raged around the giant, but Uab remained upright. At last he started to topple over. As he hit the ground he gave a violent kick with his enormous foot and pushed Peleliu far away from Angaur, where it remains today. The partly-submerged body of the fallen giant then formed islands. His legs became Koror, which has the most activity, and his penis became Aimeliik next to Koror, which today has the most rainy weather. The stomach of Uab formed Ngiwal, which is very rich in food crops, and his head rested in Ngerchelong, whose people are known for their intelligence.

And so it is today. The Palau Islands are separated, and different people have different characteristics, all because of the giant Uab who was burned and toppled, because he could not control his appetite.

Why a Girl Became a Dugong (Sea Cow) in Palau

Once there lived an old man and his wife. One day the woman went to her taro patch while her husband remained at home. While she was away, the husband was turned into a nut tree by an evil spirit. When his wife returned from her work, her husband was nowhere to be seen. She called and called for him, but could get no answer. She knew something strange must have happened and so she called the names of all the plants nearby hoping for a response. She called the lemon tree, the banana tree, the pineapple plants, the breadfruit tree and many others, but nothing responded to her voice.

The wife sat down to rest. Then she glanced at the nut tree and remembered that she had not called to it. So she gathered all of her strength and shouted loudly to the nut tree. The strength of her voice caused a branch of the tree to bow, and blood dripped down from it. The wife cried, because she knew her husband had been turned into that tree.

So the lady remained alone. Then one day she felt a stirring in her womb and knew that she was pregnant. Soon she delivered a lovely baby girl. As the girl grew up, she asked about her father. Her mother said that he had died long ago and not to worry about him.

The lady treated her daughter kindly and the girl was very obedient. The mother fed the girl all the foods available, but told her that she must never eat the nuts from the nearby tree. The girl obeyed her mother's wishes.

One day when the mother had gone to the taro patch, the girl became awfully curious about the nut tree. So while her mother busily cleared the taro patch, the girl picked nuts from the tree and cracked them. When she was about to eat the nuts, her mother suddenly appeared. The girl was ashamed for disobeying

13

her mother so she quickly put the nuts in her mouth to hide them and ran toward the sea. Her mother saw this and followed, begging her daughter not to swallow the nuts. When she reached the shore, the daughter continued running right into the sea and was turned into a *dugong*, a sea cow, and disappeared.

The girl had the nuts in her mouth but had not swallowed them when she turned into the creature. Today one can see a bulging in the jaws of the dugong where the nuts were in the girl's mouth. When one is caught, it breathes like a human, and when it is about to be killed, one can see the tears of the crying daughter flowing from the eyes of the dugong.

When a rooster crows in the middle of the night, it means that someone has died.

Palauan Belief

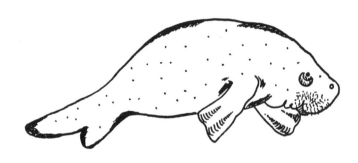

Sea Cow of Palau, *dugong*

Storyboard Carving on Palau

Palauans have always been skillful in carving, and a popular activity among the people is telling stories. It seems only natural that telling stories through carvings, or storyboards, would be a skill practiced in the Palau Islands.

Good hard woods are necessary to make a storyboard and there are several kinds grown on Palau. One is called ironwood, or *dort* in Palauan language. This wood is considered to be the best because it is strong and will not deteriorate quickly. However, it is also the most expensive wood to buy because of these qualities. Imported woods are occasionally used for storyboards, but they lack the strength of dort.

A quality carving might take weeks to complete, depending, of course, on its size. Since the tourist demand for storyboards has increased so much in the last few years, some carvers are careless and produce poor, hurried work.

When the storyboard has been carved, it will either be painted with different colors or will be treated so that the wood retains its natural colors. The painted boards are popular with tourists, but the ones that have a finish that keeps the natural shades of the wood are the most attractive. Black and brown shoe polish is used on the natural wood. This causes it to shine and the true shades of the wood remain.

The price of a storyboard depends on the wood that is used, its size, and the quality of the carving. A good storyboard may be quite expensive. Since there is no set price, it is up to the carver and the buyer to settle on the final amount. If a person is known and liked by the carver, the price could be low.

Storyboards are nice decorations for homes, but few Palauans buy them. Usually only high government officials and businessmen will be willing to pay the expensive prices. Tourists, however, find them to be most attractive. As a result, probably 90% of Palauan storyboards are sold to visitors.

The carved stories are usually old Palauan legends and are too numerous to mention. A few are as follows: *Ngirngemelas* tells about a brave Palauan warrior and his deeds; *Uwab* is about a legendary giant; *Surech ma Tulei* is a story about two lovers; and *Melechotech-a-chau* is about a giant with an unbelievably large penis.

It is not only Palauan legends that are carved, but also legends from different islands, especially Yap. To an outsider, the story that is carved is not always apparent. When a tourist purchases a storyboard, a paper is attached explaining the story.

Palauan carvers come from all walks of life, and the skill does not necessarily run in families. One of the most famous Palauan carvers, Hitler, learned his carving skill from another master carver in jail in Koror.

Hearing a gecko making noise in the middle of your ceiling is bad luck, but seeing a butterfly flying past you brings good luck.

Palauan Beliefs

Palauan Storyboard, "*Itabori*"

Customs Before and After a Funeral
on Palau

Palauan funeral customs follow a set pattern. Although all people in the community are involved in some way, immediate relatives of the person who has died have specific responsibilities.

As soon as a death occurs, the head of the clan of the deceased will notify the relatives. (In the past this was done by word of mouth, but today both messengers and a radio broadcast are used.) The relatives of the dead person, with the help of others in the community, will build a coffin and the real sister of the deceased will prepare the body for burial. The body is then placed in the coffin and put in the center of the *abai*, or community house. However, if the family has a house large enough, the body might be kept there. All people in the community will offer help, or at least appear at the abai.

The sister-in-law of the deceased is responsible for bringing food which will be served to the visitors. The female relatives of both sides of the family will help her with this, however. In return, the female visitors contribute such gifts as cloth, soaps, fine woven mats, and *toluk*, Palauan money, to the sister-in-law.

The burial ceremony takes place after one or two days, but when a chief dies it might wait up to four days. While the body is at the abai, there are specific places where the sister of the deceased sits while other relatives are sitting opposite each other. When a married man dies, the four grandparents, if they are living, sit opposite each other in pairs at the coffin. The wife's place is at the foot on one side while her mother takes the foot at the other side of the coffin. At this time, the wife is too grief stricken to be close to the head of her husband. The sisters sit at the head and are expected to place their faces close to the face of the dead brother and wail loudly in a manner that is forbidden to the wife. The wife is expected to weep, but must keep her composure.

A person is designated to serve food to visitors at this time. The chief is served first, then the women around the coffin, and then those who are outside, and lastly, those who are cooking food. Either a man or a woman from a higher clan will serve. The reason is that the server must be familiar with high clan customs so he serves the chief properly. If this is not done, the parents of the dead person might be fined Palauan money.

The chief, the father of the deceased, and the closest relative will select the burial site. Palauans have different cemeteries.

There are community, high clan, low clan, and family graveyards. After the grave has been dug by the appointed men, these elders will decide on the time of burial. It is customary to bury the dead about three to five o'clock p.m. Before burial, all the sons, daughters, and sisters will make a final visit to the body before the coffin is closed.

The coffin is carried head first from the abai, cradled in a rope sling between bamboo poles. The sister leaves the abai first, carrying two woven mats. She is followed by others in procession to the cemetery. Upon arrival, the sister places one mat in the grave. The coffin will be placed on this mat and the other mat will cover the top of the coffin. After the coffin is lowered into the grave, the mourners walk by, each dropping a handful of soil into it.

Following the burial, everyone returns to the place where the body had been kept, and food is served. After this, they are free to return to their homes. Close relatives remain for a longer period of time, however. On the seventh day after the burial, the relatives visit the grave and enclose it in cement. This is the final day of official mourning.

Layers of clouds stacked on top of each other is a sign of death.

Palauan Belief

Republic of Belau
Southwest Islands

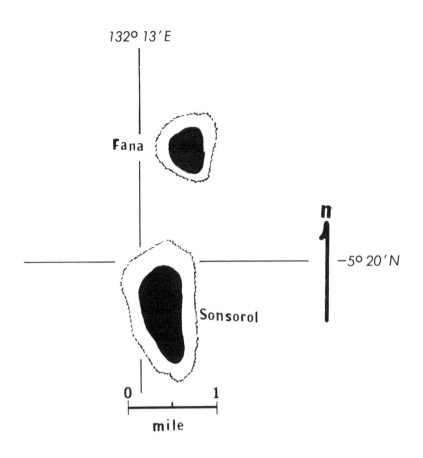

132° 13' E

Fana

n

−5° 20' N

Sonsorol

0   1
mile

Sonsorol

Land area: 0.93 square mile
Population: 79 (including Pulo Anna)
Main Cultural Group: Southwest Islanders
Main Language: Carolinian (Trukic)
Population Center: Sonsorol
Political: a municipality of the Republic of Belau

If a spider has a web under an eave, and the spider moves into the house, it means a storm is coming soon.

Palauan Belief

Courting and Marriage on Sonsorol

The Sonsorol Islands are in the southwest corner of Palau Republic. Although the islands are relatively close to the Palau Islands, and many of the people from Sonsorol live there, our customs resemble those of the Central Carolines more than those of Palau. In our marriage customs, this is evident in the similarities in searching for a partner, the marriage arrangement, and the activities that follow the actual wedding.

Traditionally, a boy is never seen in public with a girl. If he wants to be with a girl privately, he would have to sneak into her house after dark to talk to her without waking all of the household. The boy also might send the girl a message and this would be done through another girl, usually the best friend of the one the boy desires. Many visits would be necessary, and the boy would continue to contact the girl until they agreed to marry. If they ever met during the daytime, they must choose a place quite distant from the home of the girl so they would not be seen by her male relatives. If they were caught together, the least that would happen is the girl would receive a severe beating. This custom of secret meetings before marriage is gradually fading on the islands, however.

When a marriage has been decided upon, arrangements are the responsibility of both sets of parents. The boy will consult his parents first. If they agree, the parents, along with the boy, will visit the girl's parents bringing tobacco and cigarettes as gifts, and to smoke while discussing the purpose of the visit. If all parents agree, then a day will be set for the wedding. A practice that has almost disappeared since Christianity came to the island occurred when the boy refused to accept the parents' disapproval of the marriage. If the boy was very much in love and very brave, he might return to the girl's house at night and take her away to his home. Often when this happened, the girl's parents would be so impressed with the boy's daring that they would consider him to be a real man and would allow the couple to marry.

For a wedding, the boy has the responsibility of providing all of the necessities, with help from his close relatives. This includes enough food for all of the people who attend. A practice long ago that still exists to some extent today is the giving of land by the boy's parents as payment to the girl's parents for their daughter.

More often today, however, such things as money, clothes, furniture, and imported foods are given to the bride's parents.

Before Christianity reached the islands, marriages were simple affairs with small celebrations. They were made by parents' agreement. A few gifts were given and a small feast was held. Today, however, marriages always take place in the church and are followed by a large feast with lots of food and drink. The party, which always takes place at the groom's home, might continue for a day and a night.

The couple traditionally resides with the groom's parents, although this is not strictly followed today. The man, however, still has certain responsibilities. He must provide fish, breadfruit, coconuts, and fresh *tuba* for the parents and his own family. If he provides well for these three families, he will be praised on the island for being a man. If he does not care for the families well, however, he will be called a man worth nothing.

Commonwealth of the Northern Mariana Islands

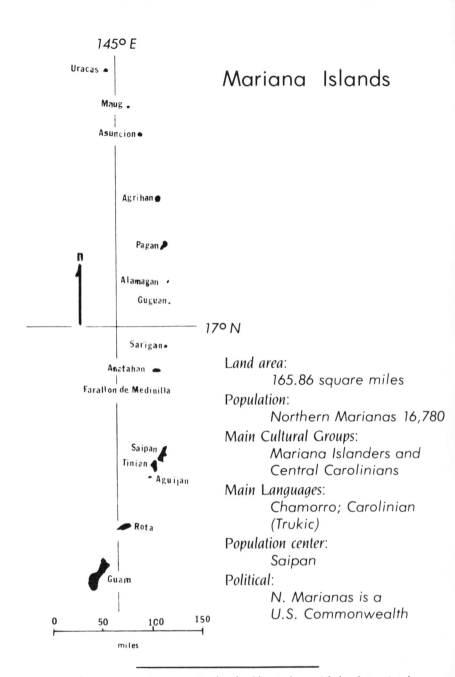

145° E

Uracas •

Maug •

Asuncion •

Mariana Islands

Agrihan •

Pagan •

n

Alamagan •

Guguan •

17° N

Sarigan •

Anatahan •

Farallon de Medinilla

Saipan

Tinian

• Aguijan

Rota

Guam

Land area:
165.86 square miles
Population:
Northern Marianas 16,780
Main Cultural Groups:
Mariana Islanders and
Central Carolinians
Main Languages:
Chamorro; Carolinian
(Trukic)
Population center:
Saipan
Political:
N. Marianas is a
U.S. Commonwealth

0   50   100   150

miles

---

*When a woman is pregnant, she should not sleep with her feet pointed
toward the door, otherwise she will have a breached birth.*

Chamorro Belief

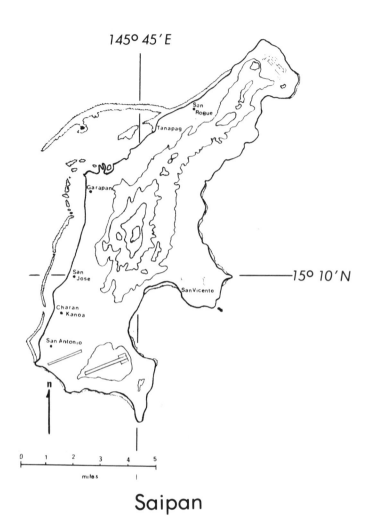

145° 45' E

San Rogue

Tanapag

Garapan

15° 10' N

San Jose

San Vicente

Charan Kanoa

San Antonio

n

0   1   2   3   4   5
miles

Saipan

Land area: 47.46 square miles
Population: 14,549
Main Cultural Group: Mariana Islanders
Main Lanugage: Chamorro and Central Carolinian
    (Trukic)
Population Centers: Garapan and Charan Kanoa
Political: part of the Commonwealth of the Northern
    Mariana Islands of the U.S.A.

Present Activities at Childbirth
on Saipan

The Mariana Islands have undergone a number of changes in administration over the past years and so it is difficult to trace the customs that have evolved since those of the original Chamorro culture. This is especially true of Saipan. A great many changes have taken place in the lives of the Marianas' people because of foreign influences. The two groups of people in the Marianas make it even harder to link the present with the past. Although Chamorros and Carolinians are similar in some ways, they are quite different in others. The differences were brought in by the Carolinians when they migrated from other islands in the Central Carolines during the last century.

Before a woman delivers a baby, there are some special activities that take place. For the Carolinians, and for some superstitious Chamorro families, a medication is necessary, especially when the woman is not married. (A woman who is pregnant without being married will have to work harder than ever so that she will not be a burden to her parents.) The treatment consists of massages and oil rubbed around the abdominal area and sometimes smoking of the woman. The latter is when the woman is covered with a thick blanket and stands over a coconut husk fire. This is conducted by a local doctor. While he is administering this, he is usually chanting quietly.

The godparents for the child will be selected from among the friends of the couple. The future parents will also be considering whether to hold a baptism party in honor of the baby.

After the child has been born, the parents will usually select his name. In some cases, however, the godparents will name the baby. The Carolinians on Saipan once gave their children secret names taken from a plant or an animal along with the names that they were called public.

If the parents decide to celebrate the arrival of the new baby, they will contact the selected godparents and relatives of both sides of the family and inform them of their plans. The immediate parents will have to provide most of the expenses for the feast, and in this they will get support from their relatives. The godparents will help, customarily, with the gift of a large sum of money for the baby.

The day of the feast is also the day that the baby will be baptized. Early in the morning of that day the parents will take the baby to the church and hand him over to the godparents. (They will be responsible for the child in case of the death of the parents.) After the ceremonies, the child is taken around and shown to all of the relatives. They will find a pouch tied to the baby's wrist and will fill it with money. At the parents' home where the ceremony and celebration will take place, neighbors and relatives will give their presents to the baby. At this feast, joy and laughter will fill the air and it will go on throughout the day and into the night.

If the parents decide not to celebrate this occasion, they would only prepare a small party and dinner for the immediate family and godparents. The baptism usually takes place one or two weeks after the child is born. If the mother of the baby is unmarried, usually no celebration will take place as they would try to conceal that the woman was even pregnant.

If a woman is pregnant, and the moon is in its first quarter, she should not look at it. If she does, her baby will be born with a cleft palate.

Chamorro Belief

Activities Before and After Marriage
on Saipan

On Saipan, as on other islands in the Marianas, it is the man who proposes marriage to a young woman. If she accepts, then this marks the time of the beginning of their engagement. The girl will then immediately inform her parents of the decision and they will decide upon a convenient date for her future husband to visit her home. When this visit takes place, all of the members of the young woman's family will be sent away except for herself and her parents. It will be the girl who receives her suitor at the door, welcomes him, and introduces him to her parents. The young man, showing respect, will take their hands in his and kiss them, saying "Niora" to the mother and "Niot" to the father.

If the discussion goes well, the parents of the girl will request to meet the parents of the young man. When these parties get together, the young man and the young girl are not allowed to be present, although the girl will be in another room and the young man will be somewhere in the vicinity. At this time the families discuss the intentions of their children. Following this, the two young people will be called into the room and questioned to see whether they are really sure of their choice and their decision to marry. Humbly and eloquently confirming their love before the parents is called *maktus i finiut* in the Chamorro language. At times, the parents will permit their children to determine the wedding date, but usually the parents will decide this. The time between setting the date and the actual ceremony is called *ma plaza*.

Weddings require financial aid for the many necessary things that will be needed for the occasion. The relatives will contribute money or whatever else they can to ease the financial burden of the couple. Most assistance is needed by the young man because he must aid the bride's family in providing a party in honor of the occasion and also contribute for another party given by his side of the family. Money or anything else given by the groom to the bride's family is called *a-uk*. The young man will also have to provide money for the bride's clothes and will buy her jewelry such as a necklace, earrings, and a wedding band.

On the wedding day, the groom and his godfather will take the bride and her godmother to the church where the blessing and wedding ceremony will take place. Since Saipan is predominantly Catholic, this, of course, would usually be a Catholic ceremony.

The celebrations following the wedding are called *fandango*. At fandango, the atmosphere is very jovial, with guests dancing, shouting, singing, and talking. It is increasingly becoming a custom to compete to see who can give the largest party with the most food and drinks provided. Following the wedding parties, the groom will take his bride to his father's home to live unless he already built a house of his own.

The above kind of marriage is the most common on Saipan, but there is another type. Two people might simply get married without relatives or friends being aware of it. This not at all common on the island, but it happens when parents disapprove of the marriage or when a young woman is pregnant before marriage.

31

Do not court, play, or cause a disturbance near a banyan tree, or the ghost Taotao Mona will punish you.

Chamorro Belief

Funeral Customs on Saipan

The two groups of people on Saipan, the Chamorros, and the Carolinians who migrated to the island in the last century, have somewhat different customs. However, the funeral customs of the two groups are very much alike.

Before a funeral takes place, permission to prepare the body for burial must be obtained from the family of the person who has passed away. More importantly, if a member of the family who loved the deceased dearly is not available, then the funeral is often delayed until the arrival of the awaited member. According to tradition on Saipan, preparation of the body for burial should be done by women. They are also responsible to dress the dead and place the body on a good, secure bed. They will light candles and place a cross above the head of the deceased.

Announcement of the death will be sent to the radio station on the island so that all friends and relatives will be notified. These friends and relatives will visit the family of the deceased, bringing with them money and flowers for the funeral. In return, members of the family will offer the guests cigarettes, betel nut, leaves and lime, and usually serve light refreshments or coffee to help them stay awake during the night. This night of the death is called *bella* in Chamorro.

The old women who are relatives of the deceased will express their grief very deeply by crying and by asking forgiveness of their faults. People will arrive to mourn with the family, especially around midnight and at the break of dawn.

Ceremonies before a burial are attended by friends and relatives of the dead and, most importantly, by a priest to pray for the deceased. By this time, the body has already been placed in a fine coffin. After this, the burial ceremony takes place. The coffin is taken to a cemetery, led by the priest and followed by those attending the burial. There are common cemeteries on Saipan where all people may be buried unless the dead person died from suicide.

Following the burial, the family of the deceased will arrange a prayer session, called a rosary, for up to two weeks. This usually is held at the home of the person who has died and all friends and relatives are invited to join the family in prayer. After the rosary period has been completed, friends and relatives come together again. On this occasion, they will donate food and money to help the family with a feast. After this, there are usually no more ceremonies for the dead until the following year when the first anniversary of the death is remembered.

The funeral customs on Saipan have been the same for many generations. No one really knows for sure about the customs on the island before the arrival of Spanish missionaries in the 16th century.

If everyone in the family is very sleepy at the same time, it means that someone in the family has died somewhere.

Chamorro Belief

Federated States
of Micronesia

Yap State

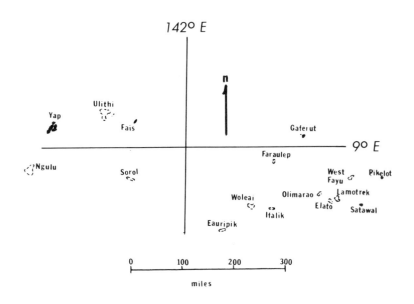

Yap State

Land area: 48.80 square miles
Population: 8,172 in 1,613 households
Main Cultural Groups: Yapese; and Central Carolinians
Main Languages: Yapese; and Ulithian, Woleian
        and Satawalese (Truckic)
Population Center: Colonia, Yap
Political: a state of the Federated States
        of Micronesia

There is wisdom in a betelnut basket. If one is bothered or indecisive, one should chew a betelnut and a calm and wise solution will be found.

From a Yapese Proverb

Yapese Inshore Canoe, ''*Thowab*''

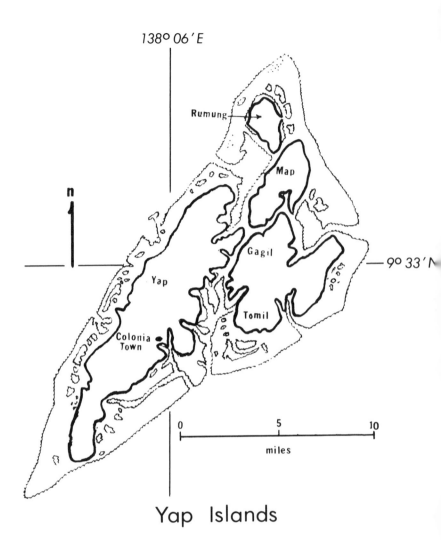

138° 06′ E

Rumung

Map

n

Gagil

Yap

9° 33′ N

Tomil

Colonia
Town

0   5   10
miles

Yap Islands

Land area: 38.70 square miles
Population: 8,172 in 1,069 households
Main Cultural Group: Yapese
Main Language: Yapese
Population center: Colonia Town
Political: center of Yap state of the F.S.M.

Don't pull up the fish trap until it is full.

From a Yapese Proverb

Traditions Involving Childbirth
in Yap

Before foreigners settled in Yap, childbirth customs were somewhat different from those of today. Now as then, however, there are specific activities and ceremonies that take place. The main changes are those related to baptizing a baby into a Christian church.

One requirement of pregnancy is that the woman must remain at home and relax and rest. It is believed that this helps the baby to be born in good health. Also, during her late months of pregnancy, the woman should sleep in a different section of the house so that she will not have sexual relations with her husband.

The husband and his family have the responsibility of caring for the pregnant woman most of the time. The husband will fish and other members of the family will gather local foods and cook for her. In Yapese custom, there are no special celebrations or feasts before the wife gives birth.

When the time of delivery arrives, it is necessary for female members of both families to be with the woman. A reason for this being that if the expectant mother dies neither family can blame the other for negligence in caring for the woman. The husband can be notified of the birth by any member present.

Members of both families will meet several days after the birth and talk about the new infant and cultural requirements for the woman. She and the infant must go to a certain place where women go during their menstruation period. Some men will accompany them, but will stay in a separate house. These men will guard the women to see that young men do not talk and disturb them. Another woman will accompany the mother at this time. She is called "*yarif.*" This woman's duties are to nurse the infant and prepare food for the mother and baby. The place where women go during menstruation is called "*depal.*" The new mother will remain there for three days and then move to another house called "*faminay*" where she will stay for nine days. Finally, after the mother regains her strength, she returns to her family home and the duties of the yarif are completed.

When they first return home, they do not visit any other families. There is a time and occasion when the husband's family will visit the wife and this is called "*malekagtir,*" meaning first trip to see the baby. This visit lifts the restrictions on the mother and she can then go anywhere in the village or municipality. When the visit takes place, the husband's family must bring Yapese shell money with them to present to his wife's father.

After the malekagtir, a party will take place. The party is in honor of the new baby, and is called "*powochug,*" meaning to cut the baby's hair. At the powochug, many different local foods and also imported foods are served. During the feast, the husband's sister cuts the baby's hair with scissors or with a sharp piece of bamboo. A few days later, another party, called "*taniyobi,*" a Japanese word meaning birthday, is held for the baby. These birthdays will be celebrated once each year. Much food is eaten at birthdays, "*tuba*" is served, and sometimes dances and songs are presented.

Adoption is very common in Yap and insures that all families have children if they want them. Yapese can adopt a child from any family if the head of the family agrees.

A particualr person determines the name of the child, and this is the sister of the husband. If the husband has no sisters, another member of his family will name the child.

There have been some adjustment in Yapese customs since the early days. However, the traditional customs at childbirth on the islands remain the same as they were in the past.

You are asking someone for something secretly, but speaking so loud that everyone can hear.

From a Yapese Proverb

Land Use and Food on Yap

The Yap Islands are 38 1/2 square miles in area. Only Pohnpei, Kosrae, Palau, and Saipan are larger in land area in Micronesia. As a result of this, crops are very important to the Yapese.

The vegetation of Yap is similar to that of the other high islands of Micronesia. Mangrove swamps exist along most of the shoreline and coconut groves appear beyond the swamps. Also, the swamps extend inland for some distance in valleys on the coastline. The vegetation on the hills is mixed and many of the hillsides and valleys consist of forests, bush, grasslands, and coconut palms. Large forest trees grow up to 75 feet in height in the valleys and about 40 feet tall on the mountain tops. Grassland covers large portions of the hills and flatlands. This grass is burned off during the dry seasons causing much soil erosion.

The land of Yap provides an abundance of food, but the Yapese economy remains mostly at the subsistence level. The main occupations of the people are gardening, harvesting, and fishing. The popular foods grown on Yap are taro, yams, sweet potatoes, bananas, breadfruit, papaya, oranges, cassava, coconuts, pineapples, along with tobacco. Chickens and pigs are raised by the people, but these are usually saved to be eaten at feasts.

The farming system of Yap resembles that of some other high islands in Micronesia. Cultivation in the hills and the uplands is usually done by individual families in small plots. These are used for only one year at a time, and after the year is passed, the farmer usually finds another plot. These plots are scattered throughout the islands. The main food in the Yapese diet is taro, and many scattered areas in the valleys are prepared for swamp taro, or wet-land taro. Normally, shifting cultivation of taro is not practiced because it is not necessary to leave the land fallow. Taro growing can be continued by the addition of quantities or organic matter year after year. Most of the crops that are grown are consumed locally. Some do go to market for sale, but only a small amount is exported.

In Yap, a complicated system of land ownership and rights has evolved. There is no common land to be farmed. Many land owners have tenants who pay no rent and make a subsistence living from the land. But these farmers are obliged to give the land owner something if the crops are raised for a profit. Selling of land is almost unknown to the people and most property changes hands only through inheritance. In the caste system of Yap, the higher castes own the land and the lower castes usually farm it.

In addition to farming, Yapese are excellent fishermen. With the crops grown on the land and the fish caught every day, Yapese are fortunate to have a varied diet throughout the year.

Just because the taro is big, doesn't mean that it is mature.

From a Yapese Proverb

Tuba in Yap

In Yap state, a very popular intoxicating drink served at feasts and other social occasions is called *tuba*. This drink is made from coconut trees and the liquid is taken from the young, flowering coconut spathe.

To make tuba, first a string is tied around the young spathe from the bottom to the top. Then, another string is tied around the middle of it with an end tied to a coconut frond. The spathe is then sliced, but one must be careful to avoid cutting the strings around it. The spathes must be recut three times each day: once in the morning, once in the afternoon, and again in the evening. The spathe can be bent down every day by pulling the string that is tied between it and the coconut frond.

Within two or two and a half weeks of slicing, it is necessary to take a coconut shell and secure it against the end of the spathe with the mouth of the shell open to it. If the shell is placed in the evening, there will be liquid in it by morning. This is called sweet tuba, and it can be either consumed or thrown away. After another cutting, the shell is again attached to the spathe. In a few days, a liquid will accumulate that is white, and this is what makes the drink.

There is some priority in the serving of tuba when the people get together. The older people are usually served first in the circle in which people drink. Then the tuba is served around the circle

42

and those who serve will be the last to drink. Somtimes women drink, but not nearly so much as men. Children are usually not served the drink.

For some people it takes about a half of a gallon of tuba to get drunk, but the effects of the drink can be felt after only two cups. Also, all tuba is not the same in its potency. Some tuba is more intoxicating than others and some islands seem to have stronger tuba than other islands.

The greatest advantage of this drink to the people of Yap is in its price. Tuba is seldom sold. If a man has access to coconut trees and knows how to make it, he can drink for nothing and save the money that he would have spent drinking imported beer.

If betelnut juice from your mouth accidentally drips on you, it is a sign of good luck.

Yapese Belief

Marriage Customs on Yap

The traditional marriage customs among Yapese seem to have been more influenced by Christianity than other customs. Today, there are standard activities that take place before, during, and after a marriage that combine old customs with the new.

On Yap, it is necessary for a couple to get to know each other secretly, and there are ways in which contact can be made. The man will initiate the contact. One common way is to send a note through his best friend, the best friend of the girl, or another trusted person to arrange a secret meeting. Usually, the girl will refuse at least three times until she is sure of his feelings.

If, after a number of secret meetings, they decide that they would like to marry, then the man will ask permission from his parents. It is also common for the girl to speak about the marriage to her parents.

In asking for a bride's hand in marriage, the father of the man will ask a respected elder to visit the girl's parents with his son. The father will choose his most precious stone money, *Ray Ninguchol*, to be given to the girl's father. If the talks are successful, the girl's father will accept the money and give shell money in return. The shell money is to protect his daughter from being beaten. After this, the girl can be seen in public with the man and can go to his home. However, if the parents are Christian, the couple will live apart until they are married in a church.

After the couple is known to be husband and wife, a marriage feast will take place. The occasion, called M'oy, is to allow all of the relatives of the couple to give them presents. The girl's side provides food such as taro and breadfruit and the man's side will provide fish and meat. The food of the girl's relatives will be distributed among those of the man's, and the food provided by the man's relatives will be given to the girl's side. The M'oy ceremony is not very widespread nowadays. More commonly, a marriage is simply held in a church by a minister or a priest on Yap today.

Some marriages are arranged by the parents of a couple. This type of marriage insures that one set of parents will be cared for by the married couple. The man's parents will discuss the marriage with the girl's parents. If it is approved, then a date will be set for the marriage. It is the responsibility of the man and his family to provide for all of the girl's needs.

After marriage, the couple will be given a few taro patches and some land on which they can make their living. However, they might stay with the man's parents until they are able to stand on their own feet.

Marriage in Yap is very much a family affair. Although customs have changed from past times, the role of parents in arranging and approving marriages is still very large today.

If boys go with girls at night when they are young, they will have slow growth. If a young man goes with an old woman, he will get old soon.

Yapese Belief

The Magic of Yap

Magic on the Yap Islands was very important long ago and many people still believe in it. Different magicians are responsible to use their magic in different situations and some magic is used for good purposes and other magic is used for bad purposes.

One magician uses his skills for rain. It is said that when there is a drought, he can bring rain in a matter of a few days. He can also control typhoons and keep them from the islands or get rid of them when they come. His main material is a piece of stone. He knows different ways to turn the stone to cause rain to come or typhoons to leave. Another magician has special talents to deal with sickness. If the people have an epidemic disease, the elder Yapese will ask the magician to get rid of it. He will then use his powers to rid the islands of the disease and all the people will be cured.

Yapese will go to a magician when something happens to them. For instance, when someone is in trouble and a man knows the person who has caused the trouble, he will ask a magician for help. Magic will be used to solve the problem. But the man must first pay money to the magician and it is very expensive to buy magic that is used against another person. Also, magic is sometimes used by one village against another village which is unfriendly.

Sometimes a man will use magic on a woman he desires, but who does not care for him. He will go to a magician and receive a special solution which he will try to spread on the woman. This will make her change her mind and fall in love with him. A woman can also use this solution on a man if she wants him to fall in love with her.

Magicians use many materials in their work. some of these are eggs, coconut fronds, crabs, bones, small stones and plants. In making magic, magicians will first find their particualr materials for an offering to the spirit. They place the offering in a shrine while holding coconut fronds that they can shake many times. They will speak to the spirit, call on their relatives who have died, and will speak the language of the spirit rather than in Yapese.

Magic rituals take place in one of two kinds of shrines on the islands. One is called *Tocue*, which means altar in Yapese, and this shrine belongs to a single magician. It is located in a corner of his house. Another shrine, called *Taliw*, is much larger and belongs to an entire village or municipality. Taliw is not often used to make magic as it is considered to be a highly sacred place and magicians must get permission from their village or municipality to use it. Only a magician can go near Taliw.

Of the many magicians on Yap, there are five main ones. The responsibility of *Ganiniy* is to bring rain. *Trur* brings luck in fishing. *Plaw* has the power to bring success in navigation, and *Yaw* is responsible to bring victory in war. The fifth magician, *Dafngoch*, has the power to increase population.

If a man has gone fishing, and someone comes to his house and asks for him, the fisherman will catch no fish.

Yapese Belief

Traditional Yapese Money

The Yap Islands have retained their traditions from the past much more than many other islands in Micronesia. This is probably because Yapese have not been influenced by foreigners as much as other islanders have. One tradition of particular interest is the use of Yapese money.

There are five important kinds of traditional money. These are called *Mmbul, Gaw, Ray, Yar*, and *Reng*. The Mmbul money is about two feet in diameter. Gaw money is very long, the longest being about ten feet in length. Ray comes in various sizes but the larger ones are twelve feet high and twelve feet wide. Yar is shell money and also comes in different sizes. The biggest are about ten inches long and five inches wide. Reng money is quite small and is only about one foot in diameter.

The different kinds of money have different values. Among Gaw money, one called *Angumang* is the most valuable because it was the first one brought to Yap. Among the Yar shell money, one called *Balaw* is considered to be of most value. With Reng money, the largest and brightest are best. A Ray money called *Rayningochol* is valued because it was brought to Yap from Palau by raft. Among Mmbal money, each one has the same value.

Some Yapese money comes from Yap and some from distant places. Mmbul is from a municipality called *Aalipebinaw* on Yap. Gaw, however, was brought to Yap from an island we call *Ganat*, near Pohnpei. It is believed that Yar was brought from New Guinea, Palau, and Pohnpei. Ray, as mentioned, comes from Palau and Reng from Yap.

Yapese money had many uses in the past. Some of these uses are still practiced today, however. Ray, for instance, was used to buy land and some still use it for this purpose. The Yar shell money was used to buy a bride in the past and it is still used for this. Money was also used to give to others at dances. The money was not meant to buy anything, but was simply given because the people were happy.

The Yapese people are rich in cultural customs, but many foreigners do not get a chance to see them. However, any visitor to the islands will immediately see Yapese money on roads leading to a home or leaning against a house.

Whistling at night should be avoided. If one whistles at night, one will have bad dreams and even nightmares.

Yapese Belief

Yapese Stone Money, ''Machaf''

47

How the islands of Yap Became Populated

The people of Yap tell stories about various events that took place in the past. One of these concerns how the islands got their chiefs and how they were populated after a disaster.

Long ago when the islands contained only a few people, customs were strictly enforced. The whole island worshipped only one chief and the population was a mixture of people and ghosts.

The one great chief lived at a place which is still known as a high-caste village. One time the chief heard about a very beautiful lady who was a ghost and she stayed on a stone outside of the village. But she was so evasive that each time the people tried to capture her she would escape under the stone. The chief brought together all of his workers and slaves to try and find out how the lady could be captured. It happened that there was a man in the group who had his eyes in the back of his head—when he was going forward, he appeared to be going backward. A plan was made to fly kites to distract the lady, and then the man would walk up and capture her with a net, while seeming to be walking in the opposite direction. The plan worked and the beautiful ghost-lady was taken prisoner. She was then brought to the chief.

The lady's name was Leebirang and the chief was Rugog, and they were soon married. But Leebirang became very lonely in the new place and so her mother came to visit her. All of the people of Tomil, one of the islands of Yap, were told by the chief to feed the mother, who had a great appetite. They all provided her with food. Soon, however, they got tired of feeding her because she ate too much. The mother then had to steal sugarcane from the chief's garden. When the chief found that his sugarcane was disappearing, he set a trap and the mother was caught in it. This caused a great typhoon to hit the island with seas so high that all of the people were washed away except for Leebirang and Rugog.

The chief and his ghost-lady eventually had seven sons and they were distributed among seven municipalities of Yap, and this is how the islands became populated again. The youngest son was given the chief's place. In the 18th century, the chief's grave was dug up in order to find out how tall he had been. He measured seven feet and some inches, the tallest among Micronesians. A dance was composed for him that is still performed on Yap today.

Yapese have many more stories about things that happened in the past. Some people believe them literally, and some do not. But even today on the islands, stories such as that of Leebirang and Rugog are told by parents to their children and are enjoyed by the present generation.

You are getting tired like a lizard which climbs a tree for no reason.
From a Yapese Proverb

Dancing on Yap

Yapese people are known throughout Micronesia for their skill in traditional dancing. In the Yap Islands, it is not just one section of the society, one sex, or one age group who dances, but everyone should know how to dance. As soon as children are mature enough to understand dance instructions, their parents begin teaching them.

In some dances, men, women, and children perform together. In others, only men do the dancing. All dance together in the famous Yapese stick dance and the marching dance. However, a very common dance, the standing dance, is performed mainly by men and boys. When women occasionally perform the standing dance, men and boys are not allowed to participate. Dances are performed whenever there is a feast or on special occasons such as the marriage of a chief.

On Yap, men from different municipalities often compete with each other to see which area has the best dancers. The winner is determined by the dancers who follow the oral instructions given while dancing the best. Actually, a few of the dancers will be outstanding as all people do not have the same skill in dancing. Also, men and women do not compete against each other in dancing because it is said that men are better dancers, but this is not necessarily true. Women do dance better than men sometimes in the sitting dance.

In the caste system of Yap, those in the lower castes are not permitted to compete against those in the higher castes. They compete among themselves. Lower caste members are also not allowed to dance whenever they choose, but must wait for an occasion when they are asked to do so by higher caste members. There is a very common standing dance that is performed only by women in the low caste. However, there are certain restrictions. They can only perform when their chief tells them and they cannot dance in the chief's building. Whenever the chief wants them to perform, he will annouce the date and place where the dance will be held so that everyone can come and watch.

There are no different dances for different age groups. Dances are performed by people of all ages except for the very young and the very old who are physically incapable.

On Yap, dancing is one of the most important skills that can be possessed, and so all people try to improve their dancing skills. It is felt by the people that anyone who cannot dance is not a true Yapese.

Being big is only like many sections of bamboo. Strength does not depend on one's size.

From a Yapese Proverb

Yapese Dance, "*Gaslew*"

50

Two Kinds of Funerals on Yap

Rites at funerals have been influenced by missionaries on the Yap Islands in the present century. Today, there are actually two kinds of funerals. One kind is for ordinary people and the other, which is more traditional, is for magicians.

When a death occurs among ordinary people in a village, visitors from all over the area come to grieve for the dead person. They arrive bringing shell money which is given to the family of the deceased. If the person who died is male, the men present the money. For a female, this is the responsibility of the women.

When a person dies, some women are selected to keep watch over the deceased during the night. These women dance and chant in the traditional Yapese way. The man of the family is expected to give shell money to these women and also to supply them with betel nuts, tobacco, or cigarettes. It is necessary for these women to get permission to dance as the family has to pay them for this service with shell money. If the women are from a different village, the family must get approval from their own villagers before the women are allowed to dance. If the villagers agree, they assist the family with shell money for the dancers.

During the day, the family also gives shell money to those who come to mourn the dead. This mourning is continued until noon of the following day when the body is buried.

Yapese bury their dead in a woven mat in a coffin. The coffin is usually decorated and may be painted any color, but black is preferred for the occasion. This custom is relatively new. Long ago, the dead were left on platforms made out of bamboo.

In the caste system of Yap, people of low caste must dig the grave. They also carry the body to the burial place while other people, especially women, follow in procession. A special song is sung on the way which signals to people that a body is being carried. It is considered to be bad luck to meet a funeral procession so people will scatter when they hear this song. The low caste people carrying the body must not look back and must not shuffle their feet against stones. If they do, they will know for sure that they will be told to carry another body soon.

Following the burial, the dead are mourned for about one hundred days. During these months, the family of the deceased does not eat fish, does not work, and talks to no one except the members of the family.

After this mourning period, the family asks their relatives and friends for taro, bananas, fish, and other kinds of food to give as payment to the low caste people for their services. At this time, the family is free to go anywhere, to eat fish, to work again, and to talk to anyone they please.

A much more traditional funeral takes place if one of Yap's five main magicians dies. In this case the dead person is wrapped in a mat and is buried standing upright with his head above the ground. No women are allowed in the presence of the body and only the magician's sons and his assistants attend to the funeral. After burial, a son will visit the grave on certain days to look at the head of the magician. When the skull is clean and dry, he will bring it to his home where it will be kept for praying.

Many Yapese funeral customs have changed since people have become Christians. However, the magicians of Yap do not follow the Christian style.

Dreaming about fish means that a member of the family will die.
Yapese Belief

Yap State Outliers

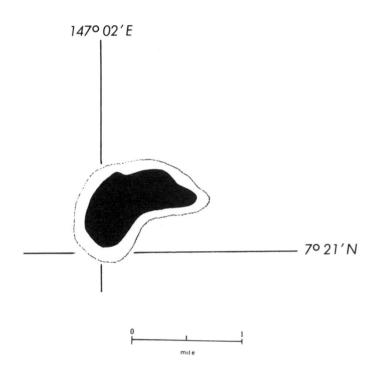

147° 02' E

7° 21' N

0   1

mile

Satawal

Land area: 0.51 square mile
Population: 386 in 79 households
Main Cultural Group: Central Carolinians
Main Language: Satawalese (Trukic)
Population Center: Satawal
Political: a municipality of Yap State of the F.S.M.

His mouth is bigger than his body.
From an Outer Islands Yap Proverb

Changing Childbirth Customs
on Satawal

On Satawal, customs followed at childbirth have changed from the times of our grandfathers. What follows are the activities that were practiced in the past. Some of these activities are still practiced, but others are not.

When a woman found she was pregnant, the uncles and her husband were notified immediately. The husband would cease cutting his hair and would not pay attention to other women. The expectant mother would be given native medicines by the uncles and the father until her last month of pregnancy, and her mother and other relatives would be responsible for providing food. The pregnant woman was expected to remain home and avoid going to taro patches until after delivery.

On Satawal, there was an isolation house for women when they were in their menstrual period. The expectant mother would be brought there by her mother and other relatives to deliver. All the women would gather around to help in the delivery and, when the baby was born alive, a loud cry would come from the group of women. The women had one particular chant if the baby was male and another if the baby was born female.

A place in the menstruation house was set up for the mother and child and one helper. This helper might be the grandmother or great grandmother of the infant and only she could enter the house. A special lave-lava made of banana tree fibers, about eight feet in length with a hole in the center, was worn by the new mother. This garment covered her from her neck to her knees and she would only remove it to bathe, usually at three p.m. or at five a.m. On the fourth day, the mother and child were removed to another small house, "*imal pallong*," where they would spend the next seven days.

During the first four days, all of the men would go fishing and half of the catch would go to those in the menstruation house. The other half would be divided equally among the fishermen. Men who were not relatives stopped fishing after the fourth day, but the husband and other relatives of the wife continued to fish until the new mother and baby were brought to their home.

After returning to her permanent home, the woman had to remain there for a month. People were not allowed to go to the side of the house where she bathed her baby "*nerong*," but were allowed on the other side, "*nefanung*," where the family gathered to eat.

The baby was named by either the father's parents or the mother's parents, but the child was usually named after relatives who had died several years ago. If one member from each family was a navigator, the child would be named after something dealing with navigation. For example, a child on Satawal was named by a great navigator after a large reef located between West Fayu and Pikelot islands. The child could also be named after someone who was alive at the time the child was born.

The two families would get together and decide on which group would adopt the child. Both families had to agree on this decision. The child would stay in the care of the original mother and father until it could walk. Then the child would join the adopters.

Changes are gradual, but changes are taking place on Satawal. The old ways are different in some respects from what women of today go through when they give birth to a baby. Modern medicines and medical practices, along with more education, have influenced childbirth practices on Satawal.

If a woman steps over her young son while he is lying down, it will bring the baby bad luck.

Outer Islands Yap Belief

Arranged Marriages on Satawal

Arranged marriages are decreasing in most parts of Micronesia. However, on Satawal, nearly all first marriages are arranged by the two families or lineages concerned.

Between the ages of 18 and 23, a man will have his first marriage arranged for him, usually by his uncle. The uncle might ask a nephew for his preference, but just as often the arrangements for a marriage will take place and ignore any preference. However, open dislike between the couple to be married would prohibit any such marriage. In addition to the uncle, marriages can be arranged by any senior male member of the future husband's lineage.

The uncle has authority to arrange a marriage and there have been cases where an uncle has dissolved a marriage. During the Japanese administration of Yap District, there was a case of an older brother arranging a marriage for a younger brother. At the time, the young man's uncle was on West Fayu Atoll working on a tobacco plantation. When he returned to Satawal, he found that his nephew had been married for several months without his approval. The uncle went directly to the mother of the girl and complained of the match. He then told his nephew that he must leave the girl, and the young man did as he was told. The uncle is not only looked upon as a wise elder, but also a representative of a lineage for the young man.

Other marriages that might take place after the first, however, are left to the discretion of the couple involved. They are not arranged and are seldom disrupted by the lineages concerned unless a possible question of incest arises. It is believed on Satawal that a man who takes a second wife as a result of being divorced or widowed will usually be of such maturity that he will recognize the best interests of his lineage. It is unlikely with his experience and maturity that he would not marry wisely.

One characteristic of our marriage customs is a minimum of celebration and ceremony. After a marriage, the husband will usually just move into the home of his wife. The following day, the man's lineage will send a gift of cooked breadfruit or taro to the lineage of his new wife. It is customary that one or two days after this, the woman's lineage will reciprocate by sending a similar gift to the lineage of the husband.

A white heron flying behind a black one means that someone will soon marry.

Outer Islands Yap Belief

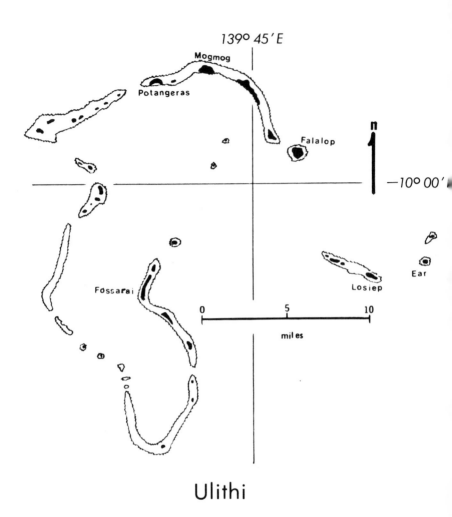

139° 45′ E

Mogmog

Potangeras

Falalop

n

−10° 00′

Ear

Losiep

Fossarai

0   5   10

miles

Ulithi

Land area: 1.80 square miles
Population: 720 in 140 households
Main Cultural Group: Central Carolinians
Main Languages: Ulithian (Trukic)
Population Center: Mogmog
Political: a municipality of Yap State of the F.S.M.

---

*If a falling leaf hits you, pick it up and spit on it and keep it. It will bring
you luck.*

Outer Islands Yap Belief

Food, Farming, and Eating Habits
on Ulithi

Ulithi has one of the largest lagoons in Micronesia. Consequently, the sea must provide much of the food for the inhabitants. However, some foods from the land are common, and these include papaya, breadfruit, wild taro, and bananas. Chickens, pigs, and coconut crabs are also eaten on the islands, although fish is the favorite food.

In addition to fish, the main foods eaten daily are breadfruit and coconuts. Chickens and pigs are sometimes eaten, but these are usually saved for feasts on special occasions such as birthday celebrations, weddings, and funerals. There are not many pigs and chickens raised on the island, so this food is much in demand.

Since fish is so important to the diet, every day and every night men will be seen fishing for their families. While they are gone, the women will prepare a soup called fe-fee to be served to them when they return. In our custom, fe-fee is always offered to returning fishermen.

The crops grown might be around the home or some distance away, depending on the size of the land. If the land is large, farming will usually be done away from the home. Both men and women engage in farming, but they have different responsibilities. The hard work of clearing the land is done by the men. The women will usually do the planting and will harvest the crop.

Families eat together in groups. The oldest son will be with his brothers and the oldest daughter will eat with her sisters. The father, the mother, and the oldest son will be served first, and the oldest daughter will offer the food to them. When bringing food to the oldest son, she will approach him on her knees to serve him. Also, this oldest daughter is responsible for the cooking, in place of the mother. Usually meals are eaten three times daily on the islands.

Feasts are quite important on Ulithi and the best foods are saved for these occasions. Breadfruit with coconut oil frosting is served in addition to chicken, lobster, pigs and fish.

If you dream of blood, and then go fishing the next day, you will catch many fish.

Outer Islands Yap Belief

142° 52' E

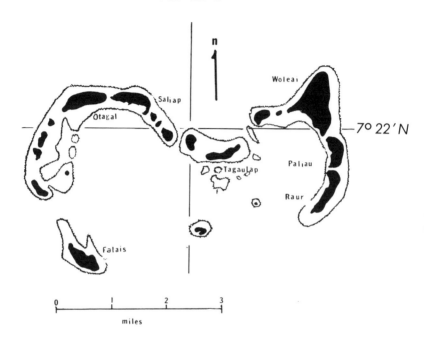

Woleai

Land area: 1.70 square miles
Population: 659 in 100 households
Main Cultural Group: Central Carolinian
Main Language: Woleian (Trukic)
Population Center: Woleai Islet
Political: a municipality of Yap State of the F.S.M.

The sea cucumber sleeps too much and does not have enough food. The eel moves and hunts and has a lot of food.
From an Outer Islands Yap Proverb

Foods and Sharing on Woleai

The land area of Woleai in Yap state is less than two square miles, and so it is necessary to utilize as much of it as possible for taro and breadfruit. Both have limitations, however, as taro requires moist soil and breadfruit is seasonal. Consequently, we eat other foods such as chickens, pigs, and dogs, but not too often. Of all our foods, fish is probably the most important.

We people of Woleai depend on taro patches to get much of our food. Our taro patches are divided into many parts and each family knows the exact boundaries of its patches. The patches are cultivated by being worked upon daily. Only women cultivate taro on our island and they seldom miss a day of working on the patches. We get food from the breadfruit trees, but sometimes this is scarce. Consequently, taro is the most reliable crop that is grown.

We eat meat mainly on special occasions such as feasts and celebrations, but our most common food is fish. The number of chickens, dogs, and pigs is small so we save them for ceremonies. Fish is a far more reliable food for us because over the years the people of Woleai have become expert fishermen. It is the responsibility of the men to provide this food and every man and boy on the island knows how to fish by various methods. Usually, the men will come together and fish in groups. When this occurs, the entire catch will be shared with every family on the island. If, for some reason such as illness, a particular man cannot go fishing that day, or there is no man present in a particular family, the fish will still be shared with these families. This is not only true of fish but of other foods as well. Sharing is most important because it indicates to us how good a person is.

There are no particular times that we set aside for eating on our island. People can eat more than six times each day if they choose, and it is not unusual to find people eating in the middle of the night if they are hungry. Also, we do not have a particular place set aside at which we eat. We simply eat outside of our houses if the weather is good and under shelter if it is poor. We do have special places for cooking, but these are used only by women. For our plates we use leaves that we consider to be better than American plates.

All of the people on my island eat well and are seldom hungry. The reasons for this are that the sea is kind to good fishermen and that sharing whatever we might have with our relatives and neighbors is very much a part of our culture on Woleai.

Two coconuts falling to the ground at the same time means that visitors are coming.

Outer Islands Yap Belief

Marriage Expectations on Woleai

Selecting a marriage partner on Woleai is not difficult for one who was born and raised on the island. In a total population of little more than 500 people, everyone knows his relatives, and is aware from childhood of the few marriage possibilities.

The status of the two families involved is not a consideration in a marriage. The most important thing is whether the two young people are closely related. Low rank within the society is also not important in a marriage and people from lower clans marry people from higher clans.

There is a great concern on Woleai about the behavior of a marriage partner. For instance, if a boy becomes engaged without the permission of his parents, they would not think the girl was the type that they would want to marry their son. Woleaians do not care about the beauty of a wife. The things considered to be important are her attitude and willingness to help others. Long ago, older relatives in our clans decided on the selection of a marriage partner. The reason the entire clan was not involved was that they might select a partner by what they saw rather than what our very close relatives might have seen. Even today, the people of Woleai are usually willing to accept the choice of their closest relatives.

The bride's family expects the man to work hard and take care of them. If the son-in-law is a navigator, when he sails to other islands he is expected to bring gifts to the family of the wife. The man's relatives only expect that the wife participates in whatever work is asked of the husband.

In the past, in traditional marriages, a large feast would take place. Some men would fish while others remained on the island preparing pigs and chickens. The women would gather firewood and baskets of taro. When the food was prepared, the relatives of the couple would apply traditional powder to the skins of the couple and put flowers around their necks and in their hair. The guests would provide two full plates of food for the couple. The couple would be told the history of marriage from times past on Woleai, and what people did when marriages were broken up. This type of marriage was practiced in the past and large ceremonies are no longer held for newly married couples on the island.

Today, in selecting a marriage partner, it is very important for the younger generation to know the history of marriage and to benefit from this knowledge. In this way, Woleaians, will follow their own customs rather than adopt those of other countries. It is important that these customs be taught to children and passed on to future generations. At present, they are taught in the home, and elementary school teachers are given extra hours to teach the children our customs in the schools.

If you peep at someone having sexual intercourse, and the woman conceives, the baby will look like you.

Outer Islands Yap Belief

Why Coconut Trees Are Prominent
on Woleai

Today Woleai Atoll in the outer islands of Yap State is covered with coconut palms, but at one time there were none on the island. At that time, there lived a girl with her mother. They were very, very poor, and were rejected by other Woleaieans and forced to live alone at the far end of the atoll. The mother and daughter loved each other dearly. The mother took good care of her daughter, protected her, and never let her play away from home.

One day when the mother left home to gather food, the girl became curious and ventured away from her house to the beach. There she saw a small eel lying helpless on the shore. The girl quickly wrapped the small creature in wet leaves and brought him to her home. She placed him in a small pond where she could care for him, but she never informed her mother about the eel. One evening her mother went to the same pond to bathe. When she saw the eel swimming, she was so shocked that she fainted. The daughter came to the pond a moment later and found her mother unconscious. She tried to revive her, but when she could not, she sat and cried because she felt so helpless. It was then that the eel spoke to the girl and told her to carry her mother home and let her rest, and to return to the pond the next morning.

The following morning when the daughter returned, the eel was waiting. He told the girl that to repay her kindness for saving his life, he would help her mother to recover, but the girl had to promise to do exactly as she was instructed. She agreed. The eel then told the daughter to return that night with a sharp knife with which to cut off his head. The frightened girl, of course, was shocked and horrified, but she had given her word that she would do as instructed. Then the girl was told to take the head wrapped in leaves to the high ground in the middle of the island where no one could see her and to bury it. She was told that in a few weeks an unfamiliar kind of tree would grow from the planted spot, and she was told that she must keep this secret from other people. When the tree began to bear fruit, she must pick the fruit, remove the husk, and find the hard shell in the center. On this shell she would see the eyes and mouth of the eel clearly visible. After opening the shell, she was told to feed the liquid to her mother, and she would awaken from her long sleep. The obedient girl did exactly as she was told, and soon her mother completely recovered.

And so this is how the first coconut palm was grown on Woleai. It also explains the secret of how the eyes and the mouth of the eel, who sacrificed his head, appear on every coconut, even today.

If a tooth is pulled out or falls out of your mouth, it should be thrown on the roof of your house to bring you luck.

Outer Islands Yap Belief

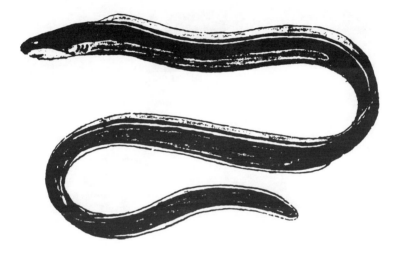

Salt-water Eel

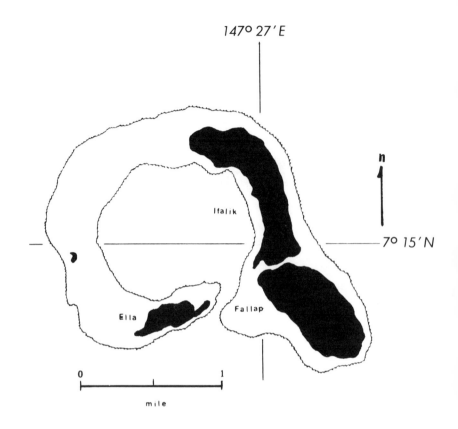

147° 27' E

n

7° 15' N

Ifalik

Ella

Fallap

0   1

mile

Ifalik

Land area: 0.37 square mile
Population: 391 in 52 households
Main Cultural Group: Central Carolinians
Main Lanugage: Woleian (Trukic)
Population Center: Ifalik Islet
Political: a municipality of Yap State of the F.S.M.

He has only the forehead, but nothing inside.
From an Outer Islands Yap Proverb

Learning Navigation on Ifalik

In the outer islands of Yap State, navigation in canoes remains a very important skill. Experienced navigators from Ifalik sail to distant islands without the use of modern instruments. They depend mainly on the ocean currents and their knowledge of the winds and stars to sail to their destinations and they hardly ever lose their way. It is known that long ago, trips to Truk, Yap, and the Philippines were frequent. Even very recently, canoes sailed from the outer islands as far as Saipan. If they lose their way, strong sailors might spend several months at sea and survive. If this happens, the captain will perform magic or say special prayers to please the spirit of navigation. Then they will reach land safely.

According to what we have been told, navigators long ago were always elderly. Today, although some elderly men are still excellent navigators, one can see a number of young men with the ability to sail to distant islands.

Learning to navigate can be either formal or informal. One way is to simply ask questions to master navigators. This is usually done in the evening while groups of men are drinking tuba. As navigation is discussed, two or three old men will join the group and tell what they know about the subject.

A second way of learning this skill is from within the family members, although members of another family might occasionally come and ask questions. The teacher is always treated with great respect and admiration. Tuba is usually brought to him so he will feel comfortable and speak for a long time.

Another way to learn is with a formal group. This takes place in either a home or a canoe house. Those who are interested will donate something, usually a lava-lava from each student, to the master navigator. The group usually meets for only four days, and so the learners have to try their best during this time. In addition to the master navigator, another expert navigator will be with the group. He is there to insure that the master teaches all of the skills and systems of navigation to the learners without making errors. At this time, the learners are not allowed to go out in the dark and cannot talk to girls.

After the theory of navigation has been taught, it is necessary to test it in practice by taking a trip to another island. At this time, the father or uncle of the learner along with a crew will accompany him to see how good he is. If neither the father nor the uncle are navigators, then his teacher will go with him.

When one is known as a master navigator on Ifalik, he is admired and receives great prestige. There are also rules he follows. He will not eat certain fish and fruits, and will not walk near the place where women go during their menstrual period.

When fishing, if you see a turtle's tail in front of your boat, you will have bad luck, but if the turtle's head is pointing toward you, your luck will be good.
Yapese Belief

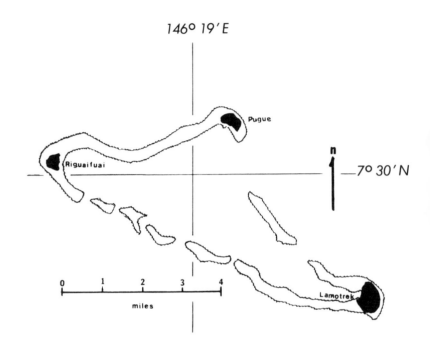

146° 19' E

Pugue

Riguaifuai

n

—7° 30' N

0   1   2   3   4

miles

Lamotrek

Lamotrek

Land area: 0.38 square mile
Population: 243 in 41 households
Main Cultural Group: Central Carolinians
Main Lanugage: Woleian (Trukic)
Population Center: Lamotrek, Pugue, Riguaifuai
Political: a municipality of Yap State of the F.S.M.

A *dragonfly in your house at night means that you are needed elsewhere.*
Outer Islands Yap Belief

Rules for Sailing to Lamotrek

Lamotrek Atoll is quite isolated in the outer islands of Yap State. Also, the population of only about 250 people is quite small. For these reasons, there are rules that all unknown canoes must follow when visiting the island.

The largest area of Lamotrek is the lagoon, which is twelve square miles in size, and these rules apply to any canoe which enters it. The first chief of Lamotrek established a policy for sailing on the island's lagoon. This policy has been enforced over many years and the younger generation still abides by the rules.

Normally, a canoe or a boat would sail all the way to land when coming to an island. However, when a canoe comes to Lamotrek it is not allowed to use sail all the way to shore. There is a shallow area in the lagoon some distance from the main populated islet. When this place is reached by an unfamiliar canoe, the sail must be taken down and the canoe paddled to the shore. This is even required of canoes from different islands in Yap State. The reason for this rule is so that the people of the island will have time to prepare for the arrival of the strangers. If a canoe keeps its sail raised and passes the boundary, then the men of the island will get their weapons ready immediately. If the rule is broken because of ignorance or a mistake, a fine must be paid by the violator.

When a strange canoe comes to the island and takes in its sail, two men from Lamotrek will go out to meet it in a small outrigger canoe to find the purpose of the visit. After this is done, they will return to the island and inform the people of what should be done in preparation for the arrival of the canoe. However, if the people meeting the canoe find that it has been lost at sea for some time and its crew is in need of immediate help, then the canoe will be allowed to use sail all the way to the shore. Those who meet the canoe will remain with it and will signal the people ashore that the visitors have been in difficulty. The islanders will then quickly collect coconuts, water, and nourishing foods for the survivors and will provide all the help possible.

Traditional customs seem to continue long after the reason for them has been forgotten. The people of Lamotrek are some of the most friendly, sharing islanders of Micronesia, so this strict rule for strangers might seem odd. It probably originated from the time of wars between islanders when strangers were suspect, but it continues on Lamotrek today.

As *sleepy as a sand shark*—*a person may be extremely quiet in manner and not say much, but when mad, he is like a sand shark which attacks and won't stop until very badly hurt.*

From a Yapese Proverb

Present Funeral Practices on Lamotrek

On Lamotrek, customs and procedures that take place during funerals today have been passed down from generation to generation.

Before a funeral, all of the relatives of the deceased will gather at the house where the body is kept. Prior to this, the mother of the person who has died, along with other close relatives, will have washed the body. The men of the family place the corpse on a mat that is covered with a *lava-lava*. All the people on Lamotrek will come to the house and one man or woman from each family will enter the house with gifts. Especially appreciated are gifts of cloth or lava-lavas. People around the house will be expressing their grief by crying and this is common for both men and women. While people are mourning, the family usually distributes cigarettes to them.

The head of the family will decide both the time and the place of the burial, but the body is usually kept overnight before being buried. At this time, men will be constructing the coffin. When this is finished, the body will be removed from the mat and placed in the coffin. It will then be taken to the church, and all of the people will go with the body to the grave site.

The grave will have been dug for the coffin. Ater the coffin is lowered into the ground, all of those present will throw flowers into the grave. The hole will then be filled with earth, and it is the women's responsibility to put new gravel on top of the grave. The relatives of the deceased will care for the grave. They will visit it early in the morning and just before dusk. After four days they will replace the gravel. During these four days, close relatives of the deceased will not work. Following these days, people will again work, but parties and celebrations will not be held for at least nine days.

A ceremony will take place nine days after the burial and this will be organized by the family of the deceased. The ceremony might be delayed to await the arrival of relatives from other islands. Before the ceremony, taro and breadfruit will be prepared by the women while the men are fishing. The men will fish for four days, or until they are sure that they have enough fish for everyone on the island because all will join in the feast. The food will be divided and every adult will receive an equal share. After the feast, cigarettes will again be distributed by the family. The purpose of this ceremony is to end the days of sadness. Following the ceremony, people will remain with the family of the deceased to comfort them and help them forget their sadness.

Traditional funerals in the past were quite different from those of the present. Long ago the dead were not buried on the land and their grave was the sea. Bodies would be weighted to help them sink, and they would be taken by canoe into the ocean for burial. The funerals of today probably date from the coming of the missionaries to Lamotrek.

Women cannot go fishing with men at night or the women will get sick and might even die after they return.

Yapese Belief

Death of a Chief on Lamotrek

The death of a chief belonging to a high clan on Lamotrek Atoll is a very sad occasion. In additon to the actual customs practiced at burial, there are some restrictions that are related to the funeral. These restrictions are a way of showing respect for the chief who has died.

After the chief has died, there is a sign, known to all of the people on the island, that is put on some parts of the reef to indicate that no one is allowed to fish there. The same thing occurs on land. *Copra* will not be made from the coconuts of some trees that belonged to the chief or his relatives. The sign consists of a stake with white coconut attached to it. The senior man in the clan will notify the relatives about which lands are not to be used.

The length of this period of inactivity is about one year, but it could be longer depending on the decision of the relatives. Some of the men from the clan of the dead chief will check the lands to make sure that no one goes to the area and steals the coconuts. The lands will be checked every two weeks or so.

When it has been decided that the people can again use the land, the senior man in the clan will notify the other chiefs. One of the chiefs will also notify the people and this will initiate a large feast. Early the next morning, the women will go to the patches to collect taro and the men will fish from the dead chief's reef. All of the fish will be brought to the men's house of the former chief's clan. After resting, the men will go to the restricted area of the land and gather coconuts. These will be brought to the men's house while the women finish cooking the taro.

The celebration usually takes place at about four p.m., as the preparation takes most of the day. When the women have finished cooking, all of the people will gather at the men's house for a ceremony. The senior man will stand and thank the people for their hard work and cooperation. Then, a chief will stand and speak. He will be given a special *mwaramwar* to place on the senior man's head to indicate to all that a new chief has been chosen. Then the feast will begin. From this time onward, copra can be made from the coconuts on the land of the former chief and men can fish from the reef that was previously restricted to them.

If you dream about losing one of your teeth, one of your relatives will die.
Yapese Belief

Federated States
of Micronesia

Truk State

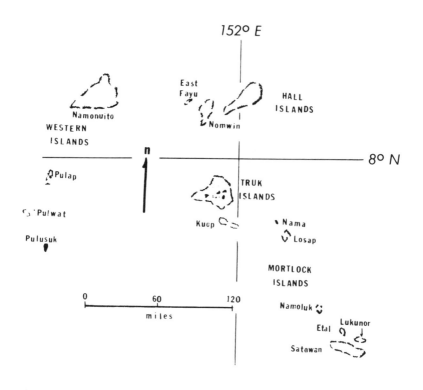

152° E

East Fayu

Namonuito

WESTERN
ISLANDS

HALL
ISLANDS

Nomwin

n

8° N

Pulap

TRUK
ISLANDS

Pulwat

Kuop

Nama

Losap

Pulusuk

MORTLOCK
ISLANDS

```
0          60         120
|——————————|——————————|
        miles
```

Namoluk

Etal

Lukunor

Satawan

Truk State

Land area: 45.97 *square miles*
Population: 37,743 *in 4,911 households*
Cultural Group: Central Carolinians
Main Language: Trukese (Trukic)
Population center: Moen, Truk Islands
Political: a state of the Federated States of Micronesia

It is bad luck to accumulate necessities such as soaps, clothing or diapers for an unborn baby before the birth of the child.

Trukese Belief

Breadfruit

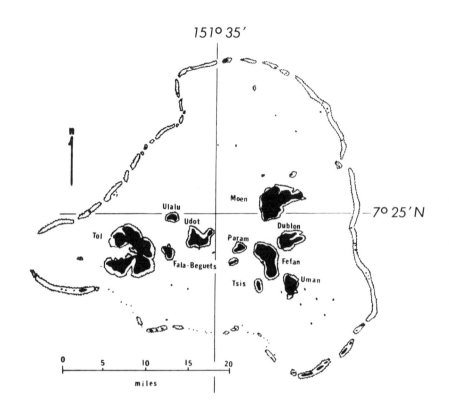

151° 35'

7° 25'N

Ulalu
Moen
Udot
Tol
Dublon
Param
Fala-Beguets
Fefan
Tsis
Uman

0   5   10   15   20
miles

Truk Islands

Land area: 38.60 square miles
Population: 28,493 in 3,569 households
Main Cultural Group: Central Carolinians
Main Language: Trukese (Trukic)
Population Center: Moen Island
Political: center of Truk State of the F.S.M.

Do not criticize someone else's behavior when you are doing the same thing you are criticizing.

From a Trukese Proverb

Changing Foods and Eating Habits
in Truk

The foods and eating habits of the people of the Truk Islands have been changing in recent years. This is a result of foreign habits and cultures coming into contact with the Trukese people.

At the beginning of the American administration, people were still very interested in raising local foods such as taro, breadfruit, bananas, and potatoes. Although men worked hard on their farms, there was little concern about having enough to eat. There was a favorite kind of food that we call *opot* in Trukese. This is actually breadfruit that has been prepared and preserved. Even though foreign foods and habits had already reached the Truk Islands, the people did not pay too much attention to them.

Local food from the 1940's and 1950's was at its best. We produced crops large enough to sell the surplus. People even organized a cooperative in which shares were sold, and this made the market in Truk successful. During the late 1960's and the 1970's, however, the number of people who care for farming has decreased. This is a result of government employment, dependence on money, and the introduction of foreign products. The emphasis on money has caused many Trukese to depend on foreign foods.

The eating habits of the people of our islands have also changed somewhat over the past years. Up until the 1960's, the eating customs were traditional and well-organized. For example, a number of people from the same family or clan lived in different places in a village. Those who prepared food would share it and divide it among these relatives. If some members went fishing, the catch would be divided and shared. During meals, the mother and daughters prepared the food for the families. When it was ready, they called the father and brothers to eat.

In recent years, however, the dividing of food among extended families and clans does not always take place. But if the family is eating and a relative passes by, the mother of the family will still invite the relative to eat or give him food to take home. Also, the Trukese people were quite accustomed to eating with their fingers. At feasts or parties people might bring spoons to eat with, but only a small number actually used them. Most people preferred the traditional way of eating. In recent times, though, this way of eating is decreasing.

There is an interesting thing about the eating habits of the people of Truk as I know them. When we eat among ourselves, it is quite customary for us to eat in the traditional manner, which is with our fingers. However, when we go to restaurants or eat with foreigners, it is common for us to use knives, forks, and spoons. Also, although imported foods are eaten often, foods such as opot are still preferred by most people.

Eating raw food before going to sea is bad luck, but a dragonfly entering your house is good luck.

Trukese Beliefs

How Land is Acquired and Used in Truk

The islands of Truk are relatively small, hilly, and of volcanic origin. They also have the largest population of any group of islands in Micronesia. Because of the small land area and the large population, ownership of land is extremely important.

There are four ways that land can be acquired today, and there are two additional ways that were practiced in the past. One way is that land might be acquired from one's extended family or lineage and another is inheritance from one's parents. Land can also be purchased with money or goods, or it might be acquired as a gift. In the past, land could be taken from a defeated enemy, the spoils of war, or it might be discovered uninhabited.

The Trukese value land as being more important than any of their possessions. We believe that if a person does not have a piece of land or two, then he is not a real Trukese. If a person has no land, he will be considered very poor and he might lose his identity and self-respect. The Trukese value land so much that fights can occur if there is a dispute over its ownership, even between relatives. The Trukese firmly believe that a man can only exist if he has land. Land is the source of food as well as wealth to the Trukese.

Besides food and wealth, land ownership has other advantages. All parts of native thatched roof houses can be made from parts of trees that grow on one's land. Trukese get fish from the

82

sea, but indirectly from the land. Without the products of the land, they would not be able to build boats and make equipment necessary for fishing.

Land can be used to validate or strengthen a marriage. Simply stated, land can buy beautiful girls. (If a man has much land, he will usually be married to a beautiful woman.) It is sometimes given as a gift to someone who takes care of a sick person; also, it can be used as a way of seeking forgiveness. For instance, if the child of one family gets cut by the child of another family, land gifts might be used as a way of settling the matter. It might also be used as compensation for infidelity. If a married woman is found sleeping with someone other than her husband by a member of her husband's family, then that person will go immediately to the woman's family and tell what she has done. The woman's family might then give land to show that they feel sorrow and shame. If there is a fight between two groups of people, the eldest member of one group might give a portion of land to settle the dispute. In other words, the Trukese say that land can settle almost anything.

Today, land provides a cash income for the unemployed. When a Trukese plants bananas, pineapples, breadfruit trees, cucumbers, coconut trees, and taro, he automatically wonders how much money he can earn from them. He will sell some of his crops after keeping what is needed for the family.

We can say, then, that land is of extreme value to the people of Truk because it allows us to live and survive on the earth. Some of the Trukese attitudes toward land, however, seem to be vanishing because of outside interference and government employment.

When everyone is in bed at night and you sneeze, it means that a member of the household will soon leave.

Trukese Belief

Past Marriage Practices in Truk

Ways of acquiring a bride have changed over the years in Truk. Today a man and a woman meet to discuss a possible marriage, although they must do this secretly. They also have more influence in the decision to marry than in the past. There used to be three main ways for a couple to be married, and in all three, parents' influence was great.

Years ago, before a man would consider marriage, he had to have experience in farming, fishing, boat construction, and had to be able to build his own house. When he was proficient in these skills, he would inform his parents that he was ready for marriage. The parents would then search for a suitable young woman to be his wife. When they decided on the girl, the parents of the man would visit the girl's parents, introduce themselves and tell the purpose of their visit, and discuss the possible marriage. If all agreed, the young man would stay with the girl's parents and the girl would reside at his parent's home until the wedding day. Prior to the marriage, both families would ready a feast to be attended by the leaders of their families and lineages. According to custom, the girl's family would provide enough food for the man's family and lineage, and his family would do the same for the girl's.

Another way for a marriage to occur was for the match also to be arranged by the parents of the couple, and this type was normally preceded by a betrothal. The custom of exchanging residences by the boy and girl also applied in these parent-arranged marriages. Among the reasons for this type of marriage were that the parents desired the marriage for political considerations or for property inheritance. Arranged marriages sometimes included more than one son or daughter. Both the brother and sister of one family might have been required to marry the brother and sister of another. Arranged marriages frequently ended in divorce because the couple was incompatible. This type of marriage still takes place in Truk today, although not nearly so often as in the past.

Another method of acquiring a bride was surreptitious and not very popular. A man would secretly give the father of the girl he desired lavish gifts. By doing this, the man made the father feel obligated to him so that it was difficult for the father to refuse his consent to a marriage proposed by the man. The daughter was then forced to marry the man.

There are some positive attitudes on marriage that have been retained from the past among the Trukese people. While both a man and a woman will desire compatible sex partners in marriage, they look even more for good workers. A person incapable of work is unlikely to be successful at marriage in Truk. There are, however, no formal marriage tests or requirements as there were in the past. On our islands, a person is well aware of the character and abilities of those in the community. A lack of previous sexual experience is expected of neither the bride nor the groom. It should also be noted that the delay before marriage tends to bring together those couples most capable of making the best adjustment in their future lives together.

If a man combs his wife's hair for her, they will soon divorce.

Trukese Belief

How Pisiiras Was Pulled from the Sea in Truk

On the island of Moen in Truk Lagoon there once lived five brothers. Before their parents died, their father called all of the boys together to talk to them. He told his sons of a lost island near Moen and said that some day they should search for it.

A few years after their father died, the five brothers set sail in search of the lost island. For three days they searched the waters hoping to find it. On the fourth day they returned disheartened to Moen. Four of the five brothers decided that their father had fooled them with his story, but the fifth brother, the youngest, still believed that his father had told the truth.

So the youngest son again set sail, without his brothers, in search of the island. After traveling a short distance, he saw that a huge shark was guiding his sailing canoe. The shark was so willing to lead the canoe that the boy thought that the fish must be the ghost of his dead father. The shark swam with the canoe until they reached the area of the lost island, and then the shark vanished from sight.

The youngest son lowered his sails and dropped his anchor. Then he dived deeply below the surface of the sea and found the

85

lost island. When he returned to the surface and boarded his canoe, he tried to raise his anchor, but found that it was stuck. He pulled and pulled with all of his strength, but he could not budge it. So finally he cut his anchor rope and sailed back to his home on Moen.

When he returned, the younger brother told the others what he had seen. Early the next day all five of the sons sailed off to find the island. When they arrived at the area, the oldest brother dove into the water and tied a rope to the island. After returning to the boat he pulled on the rope as hard as he could, but the island would not be raised from the bottom. Then the second brother tried, but even with all his strength he could not move the island. Then the third brother tried to raise the island and then the fourth brother, but the result was the same—the island could not be raised from the ocean floor. The youngest brother then tugged on the rope and the island amazingly came up to the surface. At that very moment, a black bird flew overhead and called to them. The bird told the brothers that the island should be called Pisiiras and must forever remain the property of the youngest son who believed his father.

About a mile north of Moen sits a small island all by itself. There, descendants of the younger brother still live, and the island is still called Pisiiras, the name of the clan of the brothers.

Small, but dangerous.

From a Trukese Proverb

Shark

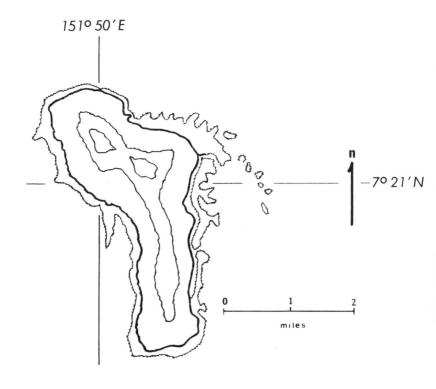

151° 50′ E

n

—7° 21′ N

0   1   2

miles

Fefan

Land area: 5.10 square miles
Population: 3,096 in 425 households
Main Cultural Group: Central Carolinians
Main Lanugage: Trukese (Trukic)
Population Center: Sapeta
Political: a municipality of Truk State of the F.S.M.

He is like a cat which is quiet during the day, but grabbing and sneaky at night.

From a Trukese Proverb

Activities Involving
a First Born Child on Fefan

When a woman has her first pregnancy on Fefan, she is prevented by her family from working hard. They will bring the food that she wants and never allow her to possibly exert herself. They will never say or do anything to make her angry or upset because this could have an effect on the baby. The husband will not make her upset and will stay with her to make her happy.

When the time comes for her to deliver, aunts from both sides of the family will come to be with her.The husband will not be present,but he will be around to know what happens. During this time food will be prepared for the woman to eat after the delivery because she will be very weak. When she has delivered, the women will shout and make noises so that the child will not be afraid of noises when he is grown up. Everybody will be happy because this is a first-born baby. After delivery, the wife's mother and the husband will make an agreement about who is to stay at the house and wash the diapers and do other duties until the new mother is strong enough to be alone.

The relatives will come and bring many gifts and also food for the mother. It is part of our culture that, whenever someone delivers, we never come to visit without bringing something, especially the husband's sisters; it is also their baby and so they will always come with presents. The couple will take turns staying with both families so that each side will be satisfied in helping to do things for the baby. When the mother and the baby are strong enough, the child will be baptized.

The baby will usually be named after someone in the family who has died and might get his name from either side, depending on the preference of the parents. If the baby is a boy, the father will give the name, but if it is a girl, the mother will name it. Sometimes, the name will begin with the first letters of the parent's name.

When this first-born baby grows up, he is the one that will be given power from the parents and relatives because he will be the oldest of the children. If he is a boy, he might become a leader. When someone in the family gets mad at someone else and he goes and tells that person to forgive, then, that is the end of the problem because no one will reject what he says. This happens with both boys and girls if they are the oldest, but it seems that the boys are more powerful because they are boys. No one in the family will turn down what the oldest son or daughter says, and this is one reason that a first-born child is so important on Fefan.

When the first birthday comes, they will celebrate it with a large feast. Both families will do what they can on this occasion. They will bring valuable gifts for the child and everyone will happy and enjoy themselves.

If a woman has a child without a husband, the parents will usually take care of the baby until it grows up. Parents, of course, do not like this sort of thing happening. At first they will scold their daughter for being pregnant, but then there is nothing more to do but accept the situation. If possible, they will encourage the girl to marry the father of the child. If they cannot marry, they will wait until the girl delivers so that they can take care of the baby. The decision of who takes care of the baby belongs to the girl's parents. There is actually no difference if a baby is born without a father. Everybody in the family will love the child and treat it equally with the rest of the children.

Many of these traditional ways are still being practiced, but foreign cultures have changed them for some people. The traditional ways seem to be more effective because they emphasize cooperation and everyone works together. The traditional ways are practiced on Fefan, especially in my village, and I believe that they are the best.

A pregnant woman should not walk around with food in her mouth. If she does, she will have a difficult time delivering her baby.

Trukese Belief

Traditional Methods of Farming
on Fefan

Traditional methods of farming and customs, although not used extensively on Fefan, have not been forgotten by the people.

The first step in farming would be the clearing of the land, and this was done by one of two methods. One method, termed *ottot* in Trukese, involved cutting out the bush and high grass. A stick of wild orange-wood was used for this purpose, and this implement was called *atter*. It was grasped in both hands and wielded back and forth like a sword. European contact introduced tools of metal that are used universally for this purpose today. The other method, *ke-ek*, involved burning the bush off the land, and this method has been widely used since the German times on Fefan. The burning was done from December to February, and planting would begin a few weeks later.

Some traditional farming methods are still used today. Once the land is cleared, planting is done with a digging stick, called *wot*. Holes for plants are made and the ground immediately surrounding the plant is turned over. Most crops are propagated by cutting a shoot from the parent root. This shoot should be two or three feet high for breadfruit and contain some leaves. It is then planted with a few inches of its stem under the ground. Swamp taro is also increased by means of a shoot called *inin*. This shoot must be at least 18 inches high or it will not survive the transplanting. A banana tree that is exhausted is simply cut down and new shoots are left to take its place. For coconut trees to propagate, a nut must be planted, preferably with milk inside. When the nut has produced a shoot a foot high, it may be transplanted if desired. A tobacco crop is increased by scattering seeds on the ground which take root. The resulting plants are later thinned out by transplanting.

When a particular crop has been harvested, the land is not immediately used again, although the time in which the land is left fallow seems to vary. For an upland taro crop, the land is left fallow immediately after harvesting. At the other extreme, banana shoots can grow in the same place as the parent tree. Certain crops such as taro, tobacco, and sugar cane require varying amounts of moisture. Because of abundant moisture in the soil, swamp taro does not require rotation, whereas upland areas become rapidly depleted. A moisture-depleted condition is referred as *mo-os-uo* in Trukese. Sweet potatoes, bananas, and breadfruit produce year after year in the same soil with little or no moisture depletion.

Many of the crops grown on Fefan today were also grown by our great grandfathers. However, farming methods are a combination of the traditional and the modern. Many old methods are still practiced, but modern metal implements have taken the place of the wooden tools of the past.

Food is for survival, and so one should never be in a hurry while preparing food or eating.

From a Trukese Proverb

Common Fishing Methods of Fefan

Truk has the second longest coral reef in the world. As a result, the fishing activities of the people include reef fishing and lagoon fishing in addition to deep-sea fishing. Traditional methods of fishing are still practiced, but modern equipment has improved them. Also, the role of men and women in fishing has changed somewhat over the years.

In former times, women fished only shallow water areas while men fished areas further offshore. The shallow area, called *neefat* in Trukese, is where small fish are caught using paired hand nets. The traditional fishing activities of men took them further offshore and they ranged beyond the barrier reef on extended expeditions. Men also fished the deep water of the lagoon and the passes in the reef. They also operated within the neefat area for certain kinds of net and trap fishing.

The sex difference in fishing activities was far more marked in the past than at present. New methods and equipment introduced by foreigners have led to modifications of the old pattern. As a result, various techniques made possible by the introduction of the metal spear and underwater goggles are today followed by both sexes, both inshore and offshore. Also, it is not unusual at present for women to accompany men to the barrier reef for fishing.

One common method of fishing traditionally is called stick fishing. A stick of mangrove wood served in former times to catch the fish, *ikeniwon*. This method, called *tuufey* in Trukese, is used at night by groups of men and women with lights or torches for illumination. In the past, the men would be equipped with mangrove sticks, but these have been replaced by metal spears. The women carry paired hand nets. A party with this equipment goes out on the fringing reef and the women surround an area of coral with their nets. Then the men poke and pound the coral with their sticks or spears. This disturbance causes the fish to dart outward and upward into the nets.

Another common fishing method also used in other areas of Micronesia is called deep water line-fishing. In this method, a hand line called *efief* is used. From one to three men go in a small fishing canoe to the deep water beyond the fringing reef known as *nemattau*. Large fish such as sea bass and tuna are caught by line-fishing. The line is weighted with a small stone tied to it in such a way that it can be jerked free once the hook has reached the bottom. The bait preferred is small bits of octopus or hermit crab.

Much fishing is done at night off of Fefan with torches. These are made from dried coconut fronds and are usually prepared during the day for the evening fishing. The number of torches prepared vary according to the time to be spent fishing. An average expedition, involving three men or women and lasting from 8 p.m. to midnight, would require about 20 torches.

Fish remains as an important part of the diet of the people of Truk, although the land also provides much food. Using nets, spears, or lines, people who are skilled at fishing are still highly respected on Truk today as in the past.

Seeing a log in front of your canoe while sailing or paddling is bad luck.
Trukese Belief

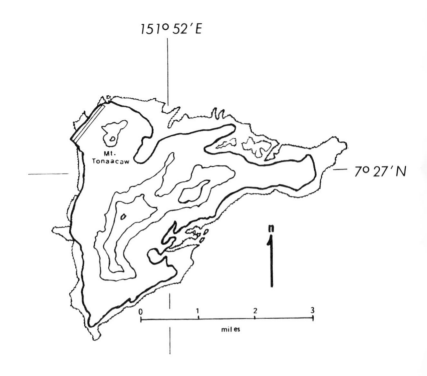

151° 52′ E

7° 27′ N

Mt.
Tonaacaw

n

0   1   2   3
miles

Moen

Land area: 7.52 square miles
Population: 10,373 in 1,301 households
Main Cultural Group: Central Carolinians
Main Language: Trukese (Trukic)
Population Center: Mwan
Political: center of Truk State of the F.S.M.

Having sexual relations before going fishing will cause one to have no luck while fishing.

Trukese Belief

Marriages and Celebrations on Moen

There are actually two main ways that a marriage might take place on Moen. One is quite common and the other is not practiced too often. The most common involved secret meetings, *tofan* in Trukese, and in this kind the couple involved has some voice in the decision to marry; the other kind is called fixed or arranged marriage. In this kind, the couple has little or no voice in the decision.

In the tofan approach, the young man first introduces his love for the girl through letters or through an intermediary. If the young man receives encouragement from the girl, he will meet her secretly at night many times. If the girl finally accepts the marriage proposal, the young man will then inform his relatives. His parents and important members of his extended family will then go to the girl's home to request the marriage. If all agree, a date is then set for the ceremony. However, if the girl's family refuses the marriage, the young man must either give up on the girl or run away with her. If he chooses the latter, they will have to hide away for weeks in the rugged hills of Moen and survive on whatever they can find for food. In the meantime, the parents and other relatives will search for the couple. If they are found, the girl can expect a severe beating from her family. At this time, the young man will attempt to prove his love for the girl by sacrificing his body to take the punishment. Seeing this, the girl's family will usually repent and accept the marriage.

Sometimes marriages will be fixed or arranged by parents without the knowledge of the two young peole concerned. Many of these marriages do not survive because there is no guarantee that the couple will get along together. There are even cases of suicide resulting from fixed marriages. Despite this, the two young people involved will almost always agree to the wishes of their parents.

Once a marriage is decided upon, there are two possible kinds of ceremony. The first one involves a church wedding. This is usually a very large ceremony which is followed by a big feast in honor of the couple. Very much food is prepared by both the bride's and the groom's relatives and there is competition between them to see who can provide the most and best prepared foods. At the wedding feast the foods will be exchanged, and those prepared by the bride's relatives will be eaten by the groom's family, while his relatives provide food eaten by the bride's family. Another kind of ceremony is a very small one. The marrying couple would simply invite a minister to conduct a marriage ceremony. Only family members and a few friends would attend. The ceremony would then be followed by a small feast. Whether the marriage is tofan or arranged, and regardless of the kind of ceremony, the bride and groom will live at the home of the husband's parents.

American customs have influenced Trukese in many ways. However, such customs as dating, or even being seen with a young woman other than a relative in public are foreign to us. Also, parents' decisions are still very important in our marriages today as they were in the past.

When a young woman wears an old mwaramwar, it will cause her to marry an old man.

Trukese Belief

House Construction on Moen

On Moen Island there are three main types of houses built. One type has a tin roof and lumber that is imported or cut at a local sawmill. Another type of house is one built with concrete blocks. This style requires imported cement and a machine to make the blocks. Both of these types are very expensive in hiring a builder and buying materials. Another type, the traditional thatched roof structure, is still very popular because it has several uses and all of its materials can be found locally at no expense to the builder. Because of its simplicity and low cost, the thatched roof model is most appropriate for the people of Truk. Basically, five local materials are used in the construction of a traditional house.

The roofing of a traditional house is made from a tree called *rupung* in Trukese. This tree is much like a coconut palm but with larger fronds. These fronds are cut down and stacked. They will eventually be sewed together for the roof after the frame of the house has been built.

Another material used is called *asat*. This is a kind of tree that is very thin and straight and measures about six to ten feet in length. The fronds mentioned above are sewed onto these sticks for walls and roofing.

The material used for sewing the rupung fronts to the asat sticks is called *is*. This is a kind of string that is made from fiber of a young coconut tree.

On Moen there are mangrove swamps surrounding the island. The trees from these swamps are used to construct the frame of the house. They are found in all sizes and so it is just a matter of cutting the desired lengths for the appropriate purpose.

Since nails are not necessary in construction, a material called *nun* is used to hold the structure together. Nun is thick string made from the husks of coconuts by very experienced older people. This string is important as it is also used to attach the roof to the frame of the house.

After the house has been built, an important celebration takes place. On this occasion, friends and relatives are invited and they will bring food for a feast. The owner, of course, will also provide much food.

Since Moen is the state capital of Truk, many concrete buildings will be seen by visitors to the island. However, the thatched roof, traditional structure remains popular because of its many uses. These include boat houses, cooking huts, shelters for drying copra as well as homes. Also, because they can cost nothing to build, thatched roof structures are practical for the people.

A building should be built so that its door faces the sunrise, and this will bring luck to the residents.

Trukese Belief

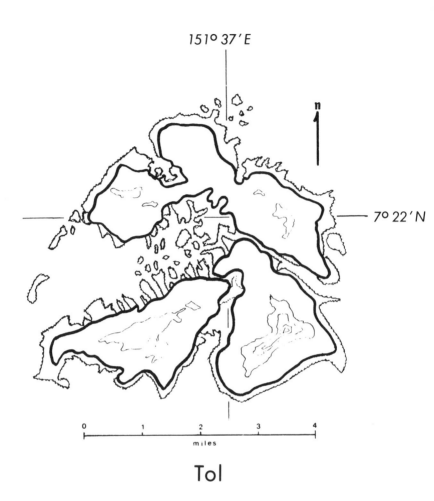

151° 37' E

n

7° 22' N

| 0 | 1 | 2 | 3 | 4 |

miles

Tol

Land area: 13.21 square miles
Population: 6,781 in 871 households
Main Cultural Group: Central Carolinian
Main Lanugage: Trukese (Trukic)
Population Center: Wonip
Political: part of Truk State of the F.S.M.

If a crab crawls into a house, it means that a funeral will take place in that house.

Trukese Belief

Activities Before and After a Death
on Tol

On the island of Tol, in Truk Lagoon, the procedure followed from the time a death occurs until after the burial is well established and understood by all islanders.

Immediately after a death occurs, a leader of the family will take charge of the funeral arrangements. He must first make sure that all relatives of the dead person are notified of the sad news as soon as possible. This person also decides on how much time is allowed before the body is buried. It is usual for the body to be kept for two days and one night. Long ago, the oldest in the clan would have these responsibilities, but today the heads of individual families are in charge. Female members of the family will usually prepare a body for burial. If the corpse is that of a married man, his wife will be permitted to assist.

There is a wake provided by the dead person's relatives and anyone from the community may attend. Some relatives will be appointed to take care of the visitors and to cook various foods while others assure that visitors are supplied with drinks and have a place to stay. Although no formal ceremony takes place before a burial, usually some young men will come and sing songs to show respect and love for the person who has died.

Grief is expressed by women through very loud crying. Men, however, usually do not cry aloud. They express grief by working very hard at cooking and making people feel at home. Some men find it impossible to control their tears and will cry with the women. When the singers begin, many people cry loudly and sometimes the father and brothers also cry at this time.

On the day the body is buried, relatives and friends will come to the place where the deceased is being kept. The pastor of the church to which the dead person belonged then conducts a ceremony. After this, the coffin is carried to the place of burial designated by the person in charge of arrangements. On Tol, there is usually a cemetery for each clan and it is common for the body to be taken there. However, sometimes the burial takes place in front or behind the home of the deceased. It is the relatives' responsibility to prepare the grave before the coffin arrives. Anyone may attend the burial. Before the coffin is buried, a short ceremony is held and then the coffin is lowered into the grave. While the relatives are covering the grave, everyone throws a little bit of dirt into it as a final farewell to the dead one.

After the burial, friends who attended will return to their respective homes. The relatives of the deceased, however, gather at the house where the dead was kept. After about one week together, these relatives will return to their homes and the funeral procedure is completed.

Rain and sunshine at the same time means that someone has recently died.
Trukese Belief

Truk State Outliers

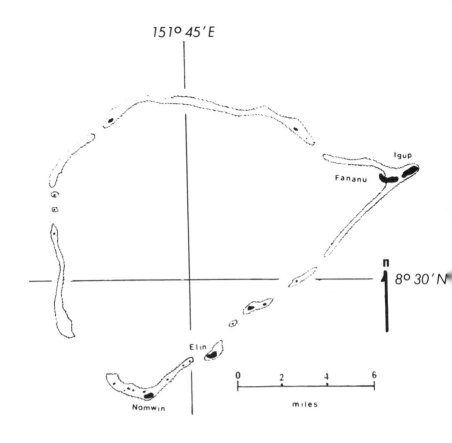

151° 45' E

Igup

Fananu

n

8° 30' N

Elin

Nomwin

0   2   4   6

miles

Nomwin

Land area: 0.72 square mile
Population: 324 in 61 households
Main Cultural Group: Central Carolinians
Main Lanugage: Trukese (Trukic)
Population Centers: Nomwin and Fananu
Political: a municipality of Truk State of the F.S.M.

*If one pays attention to an unattractive girl, it is because a woman's face is
not her only virtue.*

From a Trukese Proverb

Customs Following Childbirth
on Nomwin

On Fananu, Nomwin Atoll, no formal ceremonies or celebrations take place during a woman's pregnancy. However, there are certain responsibilities for a husband and also procedures that must be followed by families.

During pregnancy, a woman's husband will provide the special foods needed by his wife. His family and the woman's family will also assist in this as pregnancy is not considered to be a matter to handled by the husband and wife alone. The husband's role in caring for his wife diminishes upon delivery, however.

When the time for delivery is near, only women will remain with the pregnant wife. The place of delivery will even be kept secret so that the men will not know of the event. These women will include the mothers of both the husband and wife and perhaps sisters or other female members of the extended families. These women will assist the midwife by boiling water and comforting the pregnant women.

When the wife delivers and both mother and child are well, it is, of course, a time of great happiness. The women staying with the mother express this in song. If the child is a boy, they sing, "Emong chon, ukoch, ate mwan maio maio". Others, hearing this, will answer "Wuo". If the baby is female, the song is "Emon chon kinchokis maio maio", and again the answer is "Wuo". Everyone within hearing distance on the island will know that a baby has been born and will know if it is a boy or a girl.

While the baby is being breastfed, the mother's relatives will provide healthy foods. The husband must not sleep with his wife at this time. It is believed that having sexual relations soon after a birth will retard the development of the baby and it might be years before it crawls.

A large feast will be provided on the first anniversary of the birth. The families of the father and mother will both provide food for the occasion, and a favorite is breadfruit. The men will pick the fruit and prepare a large "um," or stone oven, while the women gather octopus and clams from the reef. After the food has been collected, it is taken to a large house called "ut." The two local chiefs and a priest are then notified along with the chief magistrate. These notables will present speeches and the party will begin.

and the naming of the baby are much the same now as they were long ago on Fananu.

It is quite common on Fananu for a baby to be given three names. A child might be given a Christian name and two others with special meaning. One of these might be somewhat humorous and can be given by just anyone. For instance, if a child looks like a particular old man, it will be given his name. The third name has special meaning and only "Itang" and "Palu," the navigators, can bestow this name. It has a meaning that only the navigators know.

Our customs at childbirth have changed very little over the years. This might be because our island is small and our people are few.

If a pregnant woman goes out frequently at night, her new baby will tend to cry often.

Trukese Belief

Traditional Leadership on Fananu, Nomwin

Fananu Atoll, in the Western Islands of Truk State, is quite isolated from the state center. Perhaps for this reason, traditonal leaders, or clan chiefs, are very important. The following is the way in which traditional government operates on my island.

On fananu we have two clans, and it is possible for any male member to become the clan leader or chief. The oldest man in each clan is the chief, and these two men are responsible for conducting meetings. The people give great respect to them and, in turn, they have to give respect to every member of the two clans.

The way in which the title of chief is inherited is rather simple. If my brother in my clan is my chief, it means that he is the oldest gentleman in the clan. When he dies, the oldest among those still alive will replace him. This system is true for both clans. When the next one dies, the oldest one in the clan will replace him. Myself? I will have to wait until àll the men who are older than me in my clan are dead. Then I can become the traditional leader in our clan.

The two chiefs on Fananu have great power over the people. When they have something in mind like wanting a party, they will ring a bell and every man on the island will come. The chief will then tell the men what is to be done. In this way no one can refuse. Even if one of the men feels that he cannot do what is asked, he will have to try. When the chiefs say that tomorrow we will go fishing with men and women, all the people will go, no matter what was planned for that day. When the people return from fishing, the men from the same clan as the chief will divide the fish among all the people on the island. If they catch two very large fish, these will be given to the two chiefs. The chiefs will not eat them but will divide them among his sons and daughters.

During the summer months our breadfruit trees produce on Fananu. The very first fruits that are the best to eat will be picked and given to the clan chiefs. They will be cooked, pounded, and put into a large dish made of wood and brought to the chiefs. The chiefs will then distribute the food to their sons and daughters and they, in turn, will give the food to the sons and daughters of the whole clan.

Our clans are much the same as other clans in Micronesia with which I am familiar. One outstanding characteristic of the two clans on Fananu, however, is that any man can become chief. But time must be kind to him so that he will live long enough.

Being thirsty and drinking a lot of water before going fishing means that it will soon rain.

Trukese Belief

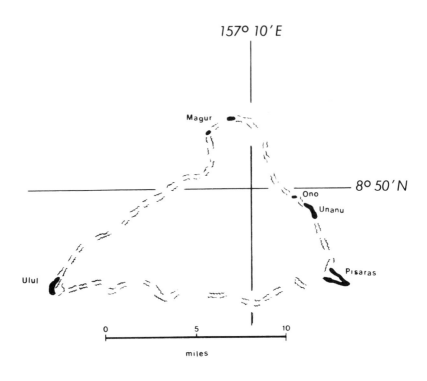

157° 10′ E

8° 50′ N

Magur

Ono
Unanu

Pisaras

Ulul

0   5   10

miles

Namonuito

Land area: 1.71 square miles
Population: 799
Main Cultural Group: Central Carolinian
Main Lanugage: Trukese (Trukic)
Population Centers: Pisaras, Ulul, Unanu
Political: a municipality of Truk State of the F.S.M.

If your eyes are itching, something will soon happen to make you cry.
Trukese Belief

Why Unanu in Namonuito is
Named After Ghosts

There is an islet in Namonuito Atoll in the Western Islands of Truk State with the unique name locally of Unanu. The meaning of the name is daughters of the ghost, and an interesting story is known throughout the Western Islands about how this place was named.

Many years ago Unanu was unnamed and uninhabited. At that time a group of ghosts had been migrating from place to place in the Western Islands in search of a home where they could permanently settle. The ghosts finally came upon this deserted island, they liked it, and they decided to remain there.

As the years passed, it became known to all of the people in the Western Islands that this particular place was inhabited by ghosts. Consequently, islanders from other atolls in the area feared visiting the ghosts' island.

A man named Olofat happened to be living on a nearby island called Weniot. He was very clever and curious, and decided to investigate the fearful island of the ghosts. So one night he left on his voyage and planned to arrive at his destination during daylight when all ghosts are known to be sleeping. When he arrived there, he walked quietly past the homes of the ghosts until he came to the house of the chief. There, Olofat was startled to see the most beautiful ghost-lady imaginable sleeping on her mat. She was the daughter of the chief of the ghosts. Olofat carefully and patiently awakened the girl and talked to her. And almost immediately Olofat and the beautiful ghost-lady fell in love with each other.

Olofat and his ghost-mistress decided to leave the island at once because they knew that the chief ghost would object to their being together. So they sailed to Weniot where they could live happily together. That night, after the ghosts had awakened, they discovered that the chief's daughter was gone. They realized that someone had taken her away, so they began a search of all the islands in the area.

The ghosts searched throughout all of the Western Islands, but they were unable to find the missing girl. It happened that Olofat possessed magical powers. When a searcher would come near his island, Olofat would turn the island upside down in the ocean so that it could not be seen. When the danger had passed, Olofat would then turn the island right-side up again.

For two years the lovers stayed together in the seclusion of Olofat's island. Eventually, though, the girl became pregnant and asked to return to her island to be with her people when she gave birth. But when they arrived at her home, they found the island to be deserted because the other ghosts were still out searching for the girl.

Soon Olofat's wife delivered twin girls. They named their daughters Un and Anu. The girls grew up and became the first people to permanently settle the island. And today, on any map of Namonuito Atoll, Unanu is clearly visible in the east as a reminder of Olofat, his wife, and the daughters of the ghost.

If a woman dreams about flowers, she will soon become pregnant.

Trukese Belief

Inshore Canoe

111

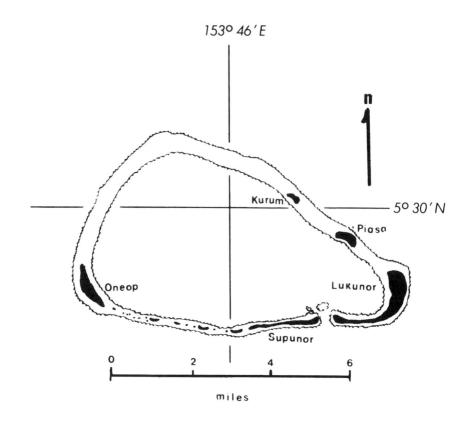

153° 46' E

n

Kurum

5° 30' N

Piasa

Oneop

Lukunor

Supunor

0   2   4   6

miles

Lukunor

Land area: 1.09 square miles
Population: 1,153 in 147 households
Main Cultural Group: Central Carolinians
Main Language: Mortlockese (Trukic)
Population Center: Lukunor, Onoep islets
Political: a municipality of Truk State of the F.S.M.

Smile at your enemy, even if deep down inside there is hatred.
From a Mortlockese Proverb

Traditional Childbirth Beliefs
and Activities on Lukunor

Childbirth is such an important occasion on Lukunor that traditional customs are followed and activities practiced. Many people believe that failure to abide by the customs and practices could result in the death of the pregnant woman and her unborn child.

We have learned from our ancestors that a pregnant woman must not walk alone in the dark or she will risk being grabbed by a ghost that could kill her and her baby. Ghosts want pregnant women because their spirits are brave, and, if they can take them, the spirits of the women will kill men, women, girls, boys and also pregnant women. This is the reason why great care is taken in protecting pregnant women.

Certain precautions are taken because ghosts are known to be very smart. They will try to fool the women staying with an expectant mother by taking on human forms and attracting them away from her. Our ancestors, though, have made something to prevent ghosts from coming near a home. It is called "*tukumoun*" and consists of leaves, stones, and secret things that are known to very few. Ghosts will not come near if tukumoun is present.

An expectant mother should not walk in the rain because of a ghost that comes only at this time to attack her. The ghost can come both day and night but it is harmless unless the woman is outside of her home in the rain. There is a ghost of the sea that can kill both the expectant mother and her unborn baby. Consequently, she cannot get close to fish when they are newly caught or the ghost might jump from the fish onto her. One weapon used on this ghost is fire. When fresh fish are brought into the home, a torch of fire is waved around them. This will scare the ghost and it will immediately return to its place in the sea.

When a woman begins to feel labor pains, her mother will be informed. She will immediately summon other women to advise and to help in the delivery. From the time of delivery, the husband will no longer stay with his wife, but will sleep and eat with other men for at least one month. He will prepare food for his wife, but he cannot come close to the house where she is staying. Our great grandfathers taught us that, if a man stays with his wife after delivery and he is called off to war, he will tremble, be fearful, and nervous. An enemy could then kill him easily. This traditional law is much respected by all of the men of Lukunor.

Great activity takes place on the day that a child is born. The relatives of the mother and father will then buy clothing, milk, and other necessities for the baby, although the infant will usually feed from the mother. The father and some relatives will collect coconuts to provide milk for the mother as this drink is a favorite after a delivery. When a large pile of coconuts is seen outside of a home, this is usually a sure indication that a baby has been born to that family.

Death during childbirth is not uncommon on Lukunor and so the day of delivery is a time of great concern for the mother and child. When it turns out that both are safe and well, great joy is expressed. The mother of the woman who has delivered will express her happiness by dancing, yelling, and she might even throw some of her possessions to the people who come. When this expression of joy is heard as a signal that all is well, people will find the husband to tell him of the good news. The husband, being so thankful, might give the messenger something he owns, such as a small piece of land or taro patch.

After a month or more the female friends and relatives of the new mother will visit her and the infant. Before they arrive they will have prepared food or acquired gifts to present to the mother and child. When they visit, they will tell stories, eat, and entertain the new baby by playing with the child and cuddling it.

Traditional custom on Lukunor does not require a feast to be held for the infant. However, today they are often held. On these occasions, food and presents are given by both the wife's and the husband's families. Also, in present times, there is often a feast right after the mother delivers. But many people on the island still believe in the traditional customs and say of them, "They are truly so," and practice them to this day.

A disobedient child who ignores instructions or commands has the ears of a turtle.

From a Mortlockese Proverb

Preparation for Marriage on Lukunor

A marriage proposal on Oneop, Lukunor Atoll, is initiated by the man. However, the families of both the man and the woman have a great influence on the decision of whether the marriage will take place.

Although initiating the marriage proposal is the responsiblity of the man, the final decision resides with the leader of the family of the woman. The man will go secretly to the woman he loves and speak with her in the hope that she will consider marrying him. If she decides that she wants the man for her husband, then he will make plans to meet her relatives to seek approval. Before this visit, the man would call upon his relatives to accompany him on this important occasion. The relatives selected must be important people in the family as it will be they who will speak for the suitor. They must know the language to use with higher people so that the proper words will be spoken.

On the way to seek approval for the marriage, the relatives will walk ahead of the young man and it is they who will knock at the door while the young man remains in the background. The first house visited would be that of the girl's family. When they are asked to enter, the spokesman will announce the purpose of the visit and discuss it with the family leader. The young man will then be questioned about his intentions and his ability to take care of the young woman. If the family leader is satisfied with the answers to his questions, he will approve the marriage. With this approval, the young man and his relatives will visit each of the houses of the other relatives of the future bride. If all of her relatives give their approval, then the marriage is accepted. At this time a sign of agreement will be made. They will shout and clap their hands, making a great noise. On hearing the noise, all of the people in the area will know that an agreement of marriage has been reached between the two families.

The following morning, the young man will go to the home of his future wife and will stay there every day. He might work at preparing food or anything else required by the family. While staying there, his own relatives will bring food to their future daughter-in-law. At the girl's home the young man is welcome to have anything he wants, with one exception. The man is not permitted to sleep with his future bride until after the wedding ceremony.

The actual ceremony is held in a church, and this is followed by a huge feast which all relatives and many friends will attend. Then the man will take his wife to the home of his family where they will occupy the same house. They can now do anything they wish and sleep together because they are accepted as being husband and wife by the people of Oneop.

The actual wedding ceremony and the feast that follows take only a single day. However, the time spent discussing marriage secretly between the couple, getting parental approval, and living together before marriage take many, many months.

If a girl chews a lock of her hair accidentally while she is eating, someone will propose marriage to her.

Mortlockese Belief

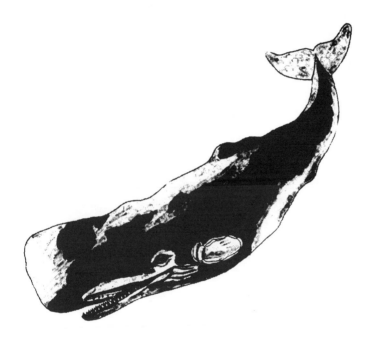

Whale

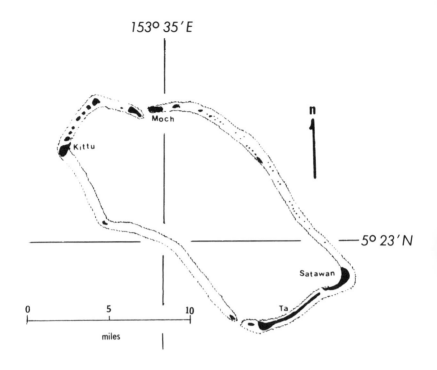

153º 35' E

n

Moch

Kittu

5º 23' N

Satawan

Ta

0   5   10

miles

Satawan

Land area: 1.76 square miles
Population: 2,166 in 311 households
Main Cultural Group: Central Carolinians
Main Lanugage: Mortlockese (Trukic)
Population Centers: Ta, Satawan, Moch, Kittu
Political: a municipality of Truk State of the F.S.M.

Don't ask for someone to serve you when the item that you want is within easy reach at the tip of your knees.

From a Mortlockese Proverb

118

Love Perfumes of Satawan

Traditional beliefs have been passed on from generation to generation in the Mortlock Islands, and are very prevalent on Satawan Atoll. One especially interesting belief is that people can be influenced in love relationships through the use of a particular perfume.

This perfume, the so-called "Satawan Atomic Bomb," is a very special substance that is extremely powerful. When applied, it can stimulate affectionate feelings in another person. However, only certain people on Satawan can manufacture and use it.

It has been known since the beginning of Satawan history that this perfume possesses the most mighty magic in all of Truk State. It must be applied with great care because it is so intolerably powerful that it can completely change a person when applied to the limbs or the face. In some cases, when not properly used, it can cause distasteful infections on the skin.

The Satawan Atomic Bomb's most important use is in stimulating love. If it is not applied too severely, it can cause an individual to have wild feelings about the person who applied it. If the perfume works properly, the person on whom it is applied will constantly think about and mention the name of person who applied it. In addition, the recipient will always search for the one who applied it and will chase after him or her.

The Satawan Atomic Bomb cannot be used by any people except the owners. However, certain members of other clans who are related to the owners now know how to make it.

The perfume cannot be used by the owners at any time that they wish. Because of its powerful and potentially dangerous effects, it requires a great deal of patience and consideration before it is used. The perfume gets the best results when a man is madly in love with a woman, and the woman hates the man so much that she criticizes him whenever they meet. If the man is willing to take his time and can find the opportunity to apply the perfume, the woman's feelings for him will completely change.

The Satawan Atomic Bomb can also be used by women on men. However, it cannot be used unless severe and insulting criticisms are being said and heard by either the man or the woman.

An outsider might think that the Satawan Atomic Bomb exists only in the imagination of the people. However, there is enough evidence of its power on Satawan today to convince the islanders that it really does exist.

When a child loses a baby tooth, take it and hammer it into the trunk of a coconut palm. The child's teeth will then grow strong like the coconut tree.

Mortlockese Belief

Funeral Customs on Satawan

On Satawan Atoll, a very loud and thunderous bell is rung when a death occurs. Either the bell at the Catholic or Protestant church will be sounded three times in succession to notify the people of the island that someone has died.

When it is known who has died, the islanders will immediately rush to the place where the body is being kept. The women will usually arrive first in order to cry over the dead person and show their sympathy for the family. In the meantime, the men will be constructing a coffin for the body. If the death occurs during daytime, the deceased will not be buried immediately, as a night must pass before the funeral. Members of the religion to which the dead person belonged will come together to have a *bedenipong*. On this occasion, people sing religious songs and give talks on religious matters in order to console the family. During the bedenipong, food is prepared by the deceased's relatives and is served to all of the people attending. The female relatives are responsible for putting perfume on the visitors, especially on the singers. They are also responsible for providing candy and cigarettes in order to encourage the singers to continue with their songs. When the bedenipong is over, the singers will be given food and will return to their homes. When the other guests have left, the elders of the family will meet to arrange the funeral for the next day.

The following day, when everything has been prepared for the burial, the body will be placed in a coffin and taken to the cemetery of the religious denomination to which the deceased belonged. Before the coffin is lowered into the grave, people attending will offer prayers for the dead and sing religious songs.

After the coffin is put into the grave, more prayers are offered by the minister or priest who is conducting the service. Then each person will take a branch, a leaf, or a plant with some soil, and throw it into the grave. The coffin will then be buried by relatives and friends while mournful crying continues. When this is completed, the relatives will place empty bottles in the ground around the grave and decorate it. While the women are doing this, the men will build a small shelter over the grave.

After these duties have been completed, relatives and friends will return to the house where the body was kept. They will stay with the family for two or more weeks and enough food is always provided for them. Two or three weeks after the burial, the family, and those who remained, will have a large feast. This is a time of sadness because the friends will usually leave shortly afterward. The purpose of the feast is to provide an opportunity for the family to express their gratitude to their friends before they leave for their homes. However, the very close relatives in the extended family will stay together for another week and then have a final feast. On this occasion, they will commemorate and give honor to what the deceased had done for them and what he had accomplished during his lifetime. At this feast, the family always encourages cooperation and kindness among members of the extended family.

Your hair will turn gray if you put coconut oil on it during a funeral.
Mortlockese Belief

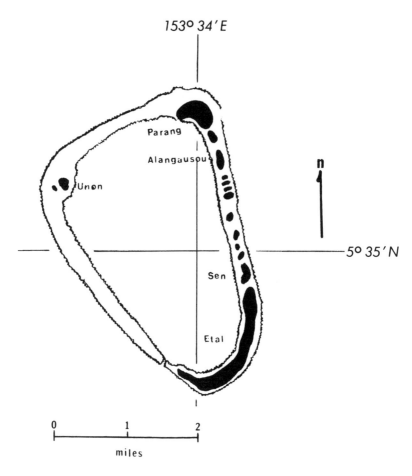

153° 34' E

Parang

Alangausou

Unon

n

5° 35' N

Sen

Etal

0   1   2

miles

Etal

Land area: 0.73 square miles
Population: 440 in 72 households
Main Cultural Group: Central Carolinians
Main Lanugage: Mortlockese (Trukic)
Population Center: Etal
Political: a municipality of Truk State of the F.S.M.

A young man is like a bat which moves quickly and quietly, hurrying from place to place, and doing all of his activities at night.

From a Mortlockese Proverb

Two Types of Canoes Built on Etal

In the past on Etal, there were many ways of building canoes, and the work would take months or even a year to complete. Nowadays, however, there are only two kinds of canoes that are commonly constructed. These types are called *waserek* and *wafatil*. The procedures used in making these two types of canoes are very similar.

Before the introduction of foreign tools used for cutting, it took very much time for canoe builders to cut the large trunk of a breadfruit tree. Some tools in the past were made from shells and the adze was made out of stone. With the introduction of metal, builders worked faster and more efficiently with axes, knives, and saws.

To construct a waserek, a sailing canoe, the canoe builder will first search the atoll for a large, strong breadfruit tree trunk for the hull of the canoe. It will then be cut down and left for about a month in order to dry out. After this time has passed, the expert builder, along with some ten assistants, will begin work by cutting and shaping the hull. (It is a custom that when the men are working on the canoe, women are not permitted near the canoe nor to walk past it.) To finish shaping the canoe might take as long as four months.

When all of the work has been completed, and before the canoe is used, a ceremony called *wuo* will take place. The owner and his relatives will provide much food at this time for the expert builder and his helpers.

The wafatil canoe, one without a sail, is built much the same as the waserek. The differences between them are that waserek is larger, it has masts for sailing, and its hull is shaped for speed. With the wafatil type, it does not make much difference if it is fast or slow. It is used mainly inshore and is propelled by poles or paddles.

With both types, the hull will first be shaped and the inside will be cut out, and then separate parts will be added. A *sia*, or outrigger, will be added to balance the canoe and an *epep* will be made in which valuable things will be kept. *So* will be carved to sit on and *au* to keep the sails secure on waserek canoes.

When all parts have been added to the canoe, the owner will set a day for *alika*, which is another ceremony held after the work has been completed. When this day arrives, the owner and his relatives will provide valuable goods and foods to cheer up the occasion. Then the men will go fishing in the canoe and all of the catch will be brought to the celebration and given to the expert builder and his helpers.

Ocean-going Canoe

It is better to dirty your hands and eat, than to be too proud to work, and starve.

From a Mortlockese Proverb

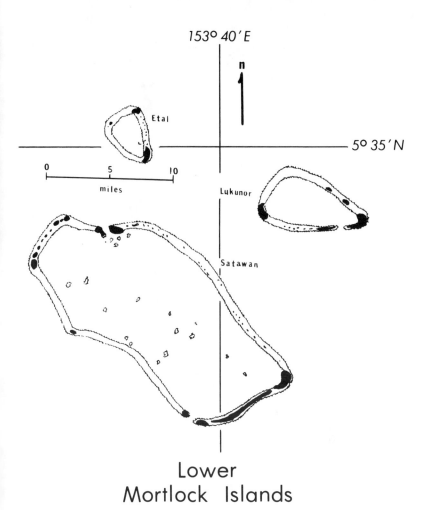

153° 40′ E

n

Etal

5° 35′ N

0   5   10
miles

Lukunor

Satawan

Lower
Mortlock Islands

Land area: *3.58 square miles*
Population: *3,759 in 530 households*
Main Cultural Group: *Central Carolinians*
Main Language: *Mortlockese (Trukic)*
Population Centers: *Satawan, Lukunor, Moch, Etal islets*
Political: *municipalities of Truk State of the*
        Federated States of Micronesia

A *person who betrays a confidence or spreads words of others is a basket*
with a hole in it.

From a Mortlockese Proverb

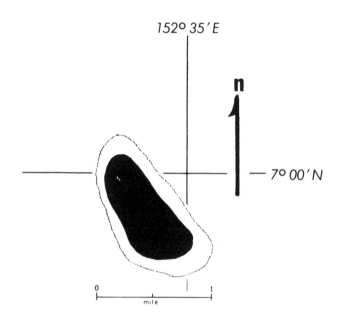

152° 35' E

n

7° 00' N

0   1

mile

Nama

Land area: 0.29 square mile
Population: 1,021 in 156 households
Main Cultural Group: Central Carolinians
Main Language: Mortlockese (Trukic)
Population Center: Nama
Political: a municipality of Truk State of the F.S.M.

If you have a boil on your leg, you will soon travel away from home, but if you have an itch in the palm of your hand, you will soon receive something valuable.

Mortlockese Belief

Family Meals on Nama

For an island of only one-quarter square mile, Nama, in the Mortlock Islands, is quite densely populated. Our main foods are taro, breadfruit, coconuts, banana, and papaya. Other foods are grown, but are not considered important.

It is the responsibility of the father in a family to collect food and of the mother to prepare and serve it. In addition to preparing the food, the mother will bring drinking water, eating utensils and dishes, if desired or available, and will wash the dishes when the meal has been eaten.

When the meal is prepared, the mother will fill dishes with food and call all of the family members to eat. When all arrive, either the father or the mother will offer a prayer to God for happiness and good fortune, and mostly for everlasting life.

When we eat on Nama, we first settle in groups whenever possible. It is customary that the father and mother eat from only one dish, while every other member has an individual dish if enough are available. No one is permitted to speak while eating, except to ask questions pertaining to the meal. If one speaks without a good reason, both the mother and father scold the person for being talkative while eating. The reason for this rule is that one who talks while eating might bite his tongue or might spit on his food, or someone else's, while talking. Another reason is that while speaking, food will not not go smoothly down the throat. This is also true of laughing, and a family member would be scolded for the same reasons as talking. These rules for eating have been passed from generation to generation on Nama and are still practiced today.

After completing our meals, the family will leave the place where they were served and only the mother and girls in the family will remain to clean up, wash the dishes, and sweep the floors.

We eat different kinds of food nearly every day except on Sundays. Fish, by our custom, should be served on this particular day. If for some reason fish cannot be caught, it would be necessary to buy sardines. We often make salted fish for this purpose.

Our meals are eaten at various times and we do not have a set schedule for breakfast, lunch, and dinner. The times depend on the availability of food, work that is being done, and the people who are preparing the food.

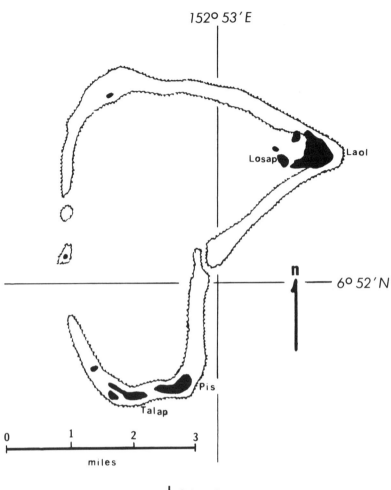

152° 53' E

Laol

Losap

n

6° 52' N

0   1   2   3

miles

Losap

Land area: 0.40 square mile
Population: 587 in ninety households
Main Cultural Group: Central Carolinians
Main Language: Mortlockese (Trukic)
Population Center: Losap Islet
Political: a municipality of Truk State of the F.S.M.

Your actions speak louder than your sermon.

From a Mortlockese Proverb

Taro, Breadfruit and Eating Habits
on Losap

We have a number of different foods on Losap. However, like most atolls in Micronesia, we consider breadfruit and taro to be our main daily foods. Breadfruit, of course, is seasonal, but we have a way of preserving it to last after the season ends. There is also a large taro patch on our atoll. In the summer breadfruit season, people will often eat both taro and breadfruit.

The summer season is the time of the hardest work for the people of Losap. We are kept busy picking breadfruit and planting in order to have enough food after the season ends. Different foods are also obtained by trade. When a farmer has a large surplus of food, he will sail to Moen or other islands in Truk Lagoon to market some of his crop. When he returns, all of the people of Losap will be called together and given some of the foods that have been obtained on the journey.

There are certain customs that we follow in our eating habits on Losap. When breadfruit has been picked during the season, people will not eat it immediately, but will await the order of the leader before eating. The leader might ask some people to prepare breadfruit for him and they are expected to do so. After the leader has been served, the rest of the people may eat. The best of the taro crop must also be presented to the leader.

Within individual families, meals are eaten together. When too much food has been prepared, some will be given to relatives or nearby neighbors. Food will not be prepared until the father orders it. When the food has been prepared, the mother will call the group together. Any member of the family might be asked to offer a prayer before eating. It is an important custom on our island to share. If anyone happens to be passing by while the family is eating, this person will be invited to join the meal. It would cause great shame to the family if this invitation were not extended.

All people prepare a great variety of foods on Losap for celebrations such as Christmas, and they all eat together. When they return to their homes, more food is served. If one family has children living in another home, food would be sent to them. This gesture would be reciprocated from the other home.

Outsiders are treated very warmly on Losap and it is considered to be an important occasion when guests arrive on our island. At this time, the leader will ask people to bring food for the strangers and the islanders will cheerfully comply. If a person fails to do so, he will be laughed at by all of the people in the community.

Foods have changed over the years on Losap, and today people can be seen eating imported canned goods. However, the idea of sharing with others remains the same today as it was in the past.

If two people's fingers accidentally touch while eating from the same plate or bowl, they must clasp each other's fingers and shake them. If they fail to do this, they will soon be separated.

Mortlockese Belief

Sprouting Coconut

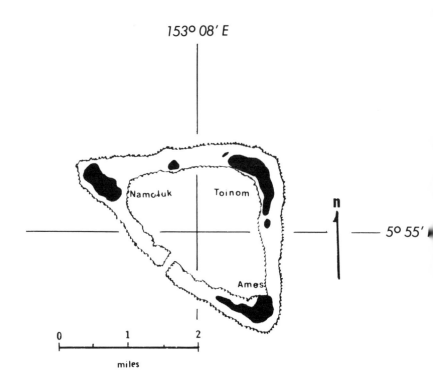

153° 08' E

n

5° 55'

Namoluk

Toinom

Ames

0   1   2

miles

Namoluk

Land area: 0.32 square mile
Population: 329 in 49 households
Main Cultural Group: Central Carolinians
Main Lanugage: Mortlockese (Trukic)
Population Center: Namoluk
Political: a municipality of Truk State of the F.S.M.

Hair cut or trimmed from a woman should be placed in banana tree so the woman's hair will grow long and silky.

Mortlockese Belief

The Lost Island of Amwes, Namoluk

Things can be seen in a certain form today, and the ways in which they came to be are often recorded in stories told on Namoluk Atoll. There is a story told about how a part of the atoll became uninhabited.

Upon the arrival of the first missionaries, Namoluk consisted of two inhabited islands called Amwes and Namoluk. However, something very unusual happened that eliminated the people from Amwes and caused it to become an islet.

It all began when a German missionary brought a minister from another island to preach more to the people about the Bible and God. However, it happened that the people of Amwes did not appreciate someone similar to themselves being their minister. The German missionary tried hard to convince the people to accept the new minister, but they refused to give in. Perhaps the reason for the natives not accepting the outsider was that they thought he might be a spy. It seems that a certain kind of fish was due to come to their reef in large schools very soon, and it was possible that the outsider was on Amwes to get this information. It is believed that the German missionary then put a spell on the islanders for not accepting the new minister. He supposedly told them that their island would turn into a place inhabited by other creatures, and not by people.

After the religious people were forced away, a *Langupwis*, one who could predict future events, told of destruction coming to the island. And it was true. A sickness swept over the whole population except for a few people who managed to escape to Namoluk. A small remnant of these people remains today, but most of the beautiful people of Amwes died from the sickness.

After this, the spell was acknowledged to be true and the island of Amwes was then used by the people of Namoluk to raise pigs. But even this did not succeed, because a typhoon in 1958 killed all the animals. Today, Amwes is only a small islet in Namoluk Atoll and only the birds make noise.

Pointing a finger at a rainbow will cause the finger to be permanently bent.
Mortlockese belief

Death and Burial on Namoluk

On Namoluk Atoll, in Truk State, a loud, desperate cry, follow-ed by the crying of many women, always signifies that a death has occurred. All people cease work immediately and the entire island goes into mourning. The only sound heard on the island is that of the women expressing their grief in crying. If there is con-versation, it is only concerned on this particular day with the dead or the family of the deceased.

As soon as a person has passed away, one of the closest relatives, usually an old woman, will clean the body. It will then be dressed in new clothes called *wou* on our island. The clothes are usually white rather than colored. Following this preparation, the deceased's male relatives will decide where the body is to be kept.

All of the elders will come to visit and pay respect to the dead, if possible. The women will be crying furiously over the body while the men are sitting in groups outside of the house talking and mourning through signs that are hardly visible. Meanwhile, a carpenter will be asked to make a coffin as the body will only re-main, at most, two days before burial.

When the coffin is built, the body will be lifted into it by men, as the women will be too weak from crying to do this. The crying will subside until the coffin is closed and then the women will again cry desperately and hopelessly. At this time, very sensitive men will cry openly.

When the coffin is closed and the grave has been dug, the mourners move with the coffin to the graveyard. This is usually on the land of the dead person's family. The only ceremony that takes place at this time is religious and is conducted by a minister. Several men lower the coffin into the grave and the service begins. This is a very solemn occasion and hymns are sung by mourners who have tears in their eyes. Prayers are also offered. Then, when the service is finished, everyone gets something such as a stone, a leaf, or dirt, and drops it into the grave. After this, the coffin is buried.

Following the burial, people will slowly and gradually disap-pear to their homes. The closest relatives of the dead person will be the last to leave the grave and they will feel great sadness. The grieving, however, will continue at home. Food will be brought by the closest relatives, but will probably be returned untouched, and words of encouragement will have a hard time penetrating. Though the idea of losing a loved one will take time to tolerate, the bereaved family will finally show their fellow islanders that they accept the loss of their loved one.

A cat crying outside of a house at night means that death is near.
Mortlockese Belief

Federated States
of Micronesia

Pohnpei State

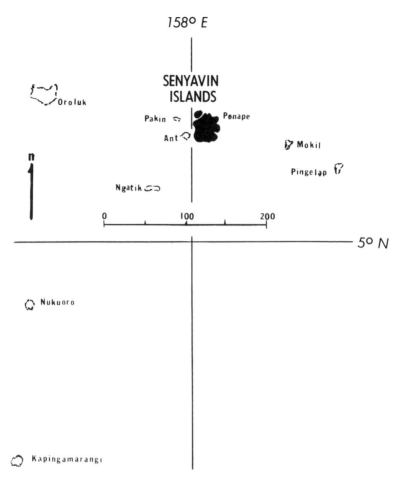

158° E

SENYAVIN
ISLANDS

Oroluk

Pakin   Ponape

Ant

Mokil

Pingelap

Ngatik

n

0   100   200

5° N

Nukuoro

Kapingamarangi

Pohnpei State

Land area: 132.18 square miles
Population: **28,879** in 3,302 households
Main Cultural Groups:
    Eastern Carolinians, and Polynesians
Main Languages: Pohnpeian and Polynesian
Political: a state of the Federated States of Micronesia

---

*We stop being an outrigger float for clansmen and become one for our father.
A father is more important than a clan member.*

From a Pohnpeian Proverb

Pohnpeian Dance Paddles, "*padil*"

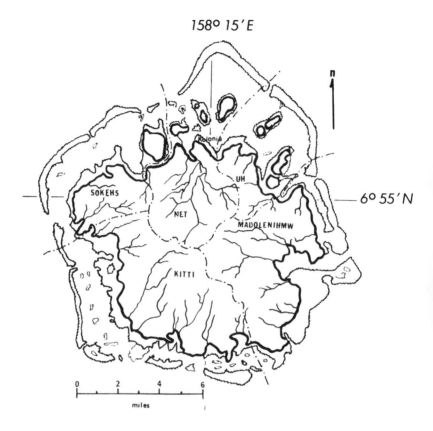

158° 15′ E

6° 55′ N

SOKEHS

NET

UH

MADOLENIHMW

KITTI

Kolonia

0 2 4 6
miles

Pohnpei
(Ponape)

Land area: 130 square miles
Population: 26,343 in 3,302 households
Main Cultural Group: Eastern Carolinians
Main Language: Pohnpeian
Population Center: Kolonia Town
Political: center of Pohnpei State of the F.S.M.

You don't have to chase the shark all the way to the reef. If your enemy wants to run away from you, let him.

From a Pohnpeian Proverb

Activities Involving
a First Born Baby on Pohnpei

Pohnpeians practice certain customs before and after the birth of a first-born baby. Some of these are traditional and have been practiced for many years, and some are of recent origin.

Long ago, when a husband found his wife to be pregnant, he would stop cutting his hair and would allow it to grow until the day of delivery of the child. This custom is still practiced by some people on the island.

A rule for expectant mothers was that they must be served a specific local medicine which is cooling to the stomach. The medicine is made from the squeezed leaves of a vine called *tehn likoahmw*. Also, the woman could not eat while walking, nor could she travel in a canoe without a cover on her. Another custom was that if she desired anything, her husband would always be sure that she had what she wanted. If this was neglected, the woman would suffer severe pain in childbirth. These customs would begin with the first sign of pregnancy and would not end until the delivery. They are still practiced by many Pohnpeians today.

After about six or seven months of pregnancy, the woman with her husband would visit the family of her parents. At this time, a feast called *kamweng kasapw* would be held. On this occasion, half of the foods would be provided by the wife's family and half would come from the side of the husband. This custom still exists on the island today and its origin is interesting. Long ago, many women died in childbirth. Kamweng kasapw was sort of a farewell feast for the expectant mother in case she did not survive the birth of her child. Today, however, death in childbirth is not nearly so common and many deliveries are handled by trained doctors.

The mother would not begin feeding the newly born infant immediately. The baby was first given a liquid called *kourapw*, a lubricant made from coconut oil. It was believed that when a child was first born, its intestines were not completely open and kourapw would help open the intestines for the mother's milk. At this time, only selected people would be allowed to visit the mother and the child for fear of transmitting diseases. The new mother and child would even bathe inside of the house.

Pohnpeians practice certain customs after the birth of the child called *pilen dihdi*. Pohnpeian *pilen* means watery and *dihdi* means breast, and the term is presently used for all things that happen after a first baby has been born. In the past, however, pilen dihdi referred only to gifts that could be consumed.

When a mother regains her strength, another ceremony called *uhm-mwin neitik* locally will be held. The person responsible for this occasion will be the husband. Foods necessary at this time include yams, breadfruit, and fresh meat or fish. Many activities take place at uhm-mwin neitik. Members of the family will go fishing for four days and will search particularly for two types of shellfish known as *kemei* and *lipwei* in Pohnpeian. These are known to be helpful for developing rich milk in the mother's breasts. After the four days of fishing, a feast will be held. Those who remained behind will contribute and prepare food while the fishermen will present their catch.

The families of the couple are expected to visit the new mother and bring gifts, and it is shameful to arrive without a contribution of some sort. This is done only for a first-born child, however. All gifts are accepted and they might include imported articles or locally made items. Some visitors might bring long, woven baskets containing a cooked pig, or dog, yams, or breadfruit. The husband will see to it that the local drink, *sakau*, is provided.

At some time following the fourth day after the birth, the mother will usually take the child out to be baptized at either a Catholic or Protestant church. After the baptism, another feast will be held to celebrate this special day.

With the passing of time, childbirth customs have been adjusted. Today, many babies are born at the hospital in Kolonia and mothers and children are treated with modern medicine. However, local medicine such as tehn likoahmw is still often given to expectant mothers and kourapw is commonly fed to newly born infants.

Family ties do not break. The ties of marriage can part, but not the ties of parentage.

From a Pohnpeian Proverb

Main Foods and Eating Habits
on Pohnpei

Because of our lush soil and abundant rainfall, there are numerous foods grown on Pohnpei. Probably the most common foods are yams, taro, breadfruit, and bananas. Among the popular meats are pigs, deer, dogs, and chickens. Fish is the most popular of all, however.

Yams are probably the most important food and they come in two types. One is called wild yam and these grow mostly in the jungles and the mountains. They are seldom cultivated and so they belong to anyone who finds them. Often Ponapeans will hunt for them when they are tired of eating other foods. The other type is planted and cultivated by individuals on their land, and this kind is the most popular. It is also the most important, because we use them at feasts and other important gatherings in the community. This kind of yam differs in color, shape, and taste, but has one common characteristic: they are all delicious to eat.

We also use banana and taro for our daily food and as a basis for making other foods. We like to save our yams for feasts, and so many banana trees and much taro are planted.

Pohnpeians consider breadfruit to be quite delicious, but its main season lasts for only about four months. These months, however, are the happiest for Pohnpeians who love to eat. It is common that during this season we visit friends and relatives to rest, have fun, enjoy parties and feast. We do some work at this time in order to have food when the season ends. Eight hours of planting can provide enough food for a week. During the summer season, we find life easy on Pohnpei.

Among other foods, many Pohnpeians prefer fish, but it is most important for a man to have pigs. These are as significant as yams, because in honoring our traditional leaders at feasts we present them with both of these foods. If a man has no yams or pigs, he will be looked down upon and not considered to be a man on Pohnpei.

We Pohnpeians have a habit of eating meals at any time that we please, and not only three times a day. At our meals you will find individuals who can consume two entire breadfruits and a can of mackerel as well. Only government employment will prevent Pohnpeians from eating whenever we please. There are also people known on the island who can finish three pounds of cooked rice at a sitting. Unlike Americans, Pohnpeians are not usually satisfied with a cup of coffee and a slice of toast at a meal. We believe that a skinny person has not had enough to eat and we praise and honor the husky ones.

Rice is becoming increasingly popular on the island, although it is imported and expensive. Presently, we usually eat rice at the first meal of the day and locally grown food at the others, because rice takes less time to prepare.

It is possible to determine a home that has an abundance of food. If a house has a lot of flies, this is an indication that there is a lot of food. No flies, no food.

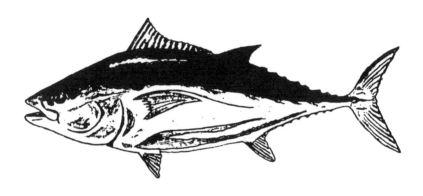

Tuna Fish

Do not invite your friends to your home before you have opened your oven.
From a Pohnpeian Proverb

Land Ownership on Pohnpei

Pohnpei Island, 133 square miles in area, is one of the largest land masses in Micronesia. It is interesting that up until the present century, only a few men, the *Nahnmwarkis*, or traditional leaders, owned all of the land.

Until the German administration of Pohnpei it was impossible for a private person to own land. Before that time, there was a feudal system of ownership. Basically, the Nahnmwarki of each municipality owned all of the land in his area and the sea that touched it. His vassals worked the land and fished the sea and gave him a portion of their farm products or their catch. Since the land and the sea did not belong to the people, this tribute was in payment to the Nahnmwarki for allowing them to use the land or the sea in his municipality.

At the beginning of the present century, around the year 1910, the German administration, under Governor Kresting, introduced the concept of private ownership of land to Pohnpeians. Under this system an individual or a group of relatives could privately hold a title to a parcel of land. A document, called a land deed, authorizing the ownership was signed by the appropriate government officials, witnesses, and the private land owner. This document took actual land ownership out of the hands of the traditional leaders.

Over the years many things have been adjusted regarding land ownership on Pohnpei including the form of the land ownership document. Also, courts exist where disputes of ownership can be settled. But the most important factor, the designating of the land to be owned by private parties rather than the Nahnmwarkis, is unchanged.

It is interesting to note, however, that in theory, the Nahnmwarkis still control the lands in their municipalities. People on Pohnpei to this day ask the traditional leaders for permission to use the land for such things as burying of the dead. Also, any visitor to the famous ancient ruins of Nan Madol is expected to ask for permission from the Nahnmwarki of Madolenihmw municipality.

All land on Pohnpei then, is owned either by private parties or government. The government land was passed on to the present administration after World War II by the Japanese and has remained in government hands ever since. Only recently, with the changing political status of the Trust Territory, strong voices are being heard to return the government land to the people.

Banana plants do not bear breadfruit.

From a Pohnpeian Proverb

Traditional Customs for Adulthood
and Marriage on Pohnpei

A number of marriage customs were practiced by Pohnpeians before the arrival of the missionaries to the island. Some have been discontinued completely while others have been blended into the customs practiced today.

In the past, the time for marriage, or the attainment of adulthood, was symbolized by tattooing of both men and women. Men usually displayed tattoos on thighs and arms while women tattooed their arms as well as their lower limbs. Neither men nor women tattooed their faces, however. Although tattoos are no longer a required symbol of adulthood on Pohnpei, they are still very much in evidence among the people today.

Among men, scarring of the body was quite common. This would usually be done with heated knives to show that the particular man had no fear of pain. It was also the custom of some men to cut off one of their testicles for the same reason. Although the missionaries discouraged this practice, there are older men living on Pohnpei today who followed this custom.

A formal marriage today is followed by a large feast where relatives of both the man and the woman celebrate the occasion. Long ago, however, little ceremony took place. A church wedding, of course, would not be held and the bride would simply be taken to the home of her husband's mother where she would be welcomed. Since all of the land on Pohnpei belonged to the *Nahnmwarkis*, or kings, at that time, the couple would reside on land cleared by the husband's relatives but owned by the particular Nahnmwarki of his section of the island.

In the past, marrying a member of one's own clan was not permitted, and this custom is still practiced on Pohnpei today. Although there are instances of it known on the island, the practice is very much discouraged and frowned upon.

A very common practice before the arrival of the missionaries was arranged marriages. In this situation the parents of a boy and a girl would determine the marriage partner. The arrangement might be made while the couple to be married were still infants, or even in their mothers' wombs, and it was practiced particularly among people of high rank in Pohnpeian society. In marriages of this kind, inheritance was usually a consideration.

Parents continue to have an influence in the marriage of their children, however. Since parents and elders are highly respected on the island, their advice and wisdom are always sought in important matters such as marriage.

Gossip is like the meaningless sounds of waves hitting the reef.

From a Ponhpeian Proverb

Present Marriage Practices on Pohnpei

Two young people desiring to marry on Pohnpei must know each other's feelings before marriage. They must arrange to meet secretly outside of their homes. These meetings continue until the couple decides that they wish to be called husband and wife.

When this has been decided, both the young man and his future wife might inform their parents that they wish to get married. Very commonly, however, only the young man will let his parents know. If they agree, then the parents plan a date on which they will visit the home of the young lady.

When asking for the marriage, the parents of the man will be accompanied by a number of relatives and will bring with them the traditional Ponapean drink, *sakau*. When they arrive at the young woman's home, they will cut the roots from the sakau plant and pound them. After the pounding, they squeeze the liquid into a cup which is given to the relative who will ask for the marriage. He in turn will offer the drink to the father of the girl, and at the same time explain the purpose of his visit. The two parents will then discuss the proposed marriage. When an agreement is reached, the young people will be called upon to join the relatives and sit with them. The girl is then asked that if by her own free will she has made the decision to marry the man. If she answers yes, then the decision has been made. When the man's relatives leave, she will be taken along with them. She is now considered to be married. After staying together for some time, and if no difficulties develop, a date will be set when they can be married legally in a church.

On the wedding day, the man's family will hold a very large party to which all their friends and relatives will be invited. It is

147

customary that everyone who attends will bring something, usually food, with them. It is very rare if someone arrives empty-handed. The woman's relatives also contribute a lot for the party, although they are considered to be special guests on this occasion. This party shows to everybody that the woman now completely belongs to her husband. She no longer belongs to her parents, and her husband now has all the rights of a married man over her.

Arranged marriages, where the parents of a boy and those of a girl decide their children should marry, also occur on Pohnpei. These marriages present difficulties, however, if the two people cannot get along with each other. It seems that increasingly on Pohnpei young men and women are being allowed to make their own decisions with the approval of their parents.

There are no taboos across the sea. Relationships not accepted by one's clan are acceptable when far away.

From a Pohnpeian Proverb

Traditional Sakau of Pohnpei

Pohnpeians have several legends about how the kava plant, *sakau,* came to exist on the island.

The young people of the present generation believe that it originated on Fiji and Samoa and was brought to Pohnpei by some early voyagers. However, old people on Pohnpei have a different belief. They say that sakau was first made by two brothers, Widen-ngar and Luhk, through magic. (Widen-ngar was a ghost who appeared in the form of thunder and Luhk was also a ghost who lived below the surface of the earth.) One day, Widen-ngar came down to the earth and joined Luhk, who came up from beneath the surface. They journeyed together from Saladak in Uh to Nahpali Island in Metalenihmw. Luhk, unfortunately, injured his foot on the way to the island. When they arrived, they took the skin from the injured foot and pounded it into small pieces. They then squeezed out the liquid using hibiscus bark. Widen-ngar took off his kneecap to use it as a cup to catch the liquid. When they finished they went to the sky and changed their skin into the form of a plant called the sakau plant. Years later this plant was found in Saladak, Uh, and the people considered it to be the most important on Pohnpei. The liquid, when consumed, had a soothing and calming effect and so it was given to the king, or Nahnmwarki, to calm him down whenever he became angry. Nothing could calm the Nahnmwarki except this liquid. From that time onward, sakau has become so important that one who owns it is considered to be a real Pohnpeian man. In the early days, only the Nahnmwarki could drink sakau as there were not many plants. Also, it could be prepared only by his relatives.

Pohnpein sakau has a most important role in traditional custom. Whenever feasts, parties, meetings, or other important occasions occur, sakau will be prepared. But preparing it is like driving an automobile, as there is a step-by-step procedure to follow. Also, there are very important rules to follow when invited to a feast. If a person is asked to help prepare sakau, the following should be done.

1. Do not bring the plant inside of the house until the Nahnmwarki is seated.
2. Cut branches from the plant and the roots into small pieces for easy cleaning.
3. Place the root on the stone and put a taro leaf beneath to protect pieces from the dirt.
4. After the root is pounded, use a hibiscus bark for bast to squeeze the liquid into a coconut cup.

Also on Pohnpei there is a priority in serving sakau and this is based on traditional rank. The first cup goes to the Nahnmwarki and the second is served the next highest leader, *Isonahnken*. The next cup goes to the queen and fourth goes back to the Nahnmwarki again. The next cup goes to those who prepared the sakau.

At present, the Nahnmwarkis allow people to sell some of their sakau, because there are plenty of the plants on the island. Drinking is somewhat like consuming alcoholic beverages. However, when one gets drunk from sakau one will not feel like moving around or hearing loud noises. Sakau is potent also. If a person drinks too much, he might start shaking, lose control of himself, and not know what he is doing.

Today on Pohnpei, people can come together and drink sakau in small bars on the island at a very cheap price. However, the most important function of the drink is serving it at traditional feasts and activities in the traditional manner.

A *sakau plant must not be placed vertically against a wall at a* kamadipw. *If the plant falls on you it will bring bad luck and even death.* Also, *bubbles in a cup of sakau will bring bad luck.*

Pohnpeian Beliefs

Pohnpeian Kava, "*sakau*"

Clans and Local Government on Pohnpei

Pohnpei is an island of many different clans and there are also smaller units called sub-clans for each clan. On the island there are four prominent clans and these have the five Nahnmwarkis of the five municipalities of the island. These clans are named *Dipwinpahnmei*, *Lasialap*, *Dipwinmen*, and *Sounkawad*. Both of the Nahnmwarkis, or high chiefs, of Nett and Sokehs municipalities are of the Sounkawad clan. Also, no other clan can have a Nahnmwarki of Uh municipality if he is not a Lasialap. For this reason, everyone who had a title on the Nahnmwarki's side or line should belong to the same clan. It is possible for a sub-clan member to become a Nahnmwarki, but this is not very probable.

Clan membership is matrilineal and so members of a clan or a sub-clan always come from the mother's side. As a result, a son and a daughter from different mothers that belong to the same clan cannot be married. In the past, this was a very strict rule, but today some of the younger generation ignore it.

The traditional government of the island is in the hands of the Nahnmwarkis. Each of the five municipalities has its own local government and contains a *Pwihn en Wahu*, a group of people appointed by the Nahnmwarki. These groups have the highest titles in each municipality and are also the leaders of the communities. The Pwihn en Wahu has all male members. When the Nahnmwarki has important decisions to make, he assembles this group. In times past, messengers would be sent to notify the members, but at present the local radio station is used for this purpose. The function of the Pwihn en Wahu is to meet with the Nahnmwarki and suggest decisions. If, however, the Nahnmwarki does not agree, he will protest at the meeting. If the Nahnmwarki needs something, he might not go through the Pwihn en Wahu, but directly to an individual. If the person cannot meet the request, he will try to find what has been asked for.

There are reasons why a request from a Nahnmwarki should be obeyed. One reason is that the traditional leaders on Pohnpei are still highly respected, although they have little real power. In the past all of the land was owned by the Nahnmwarkis and so their power was much stronger. Today, however, all land is privately owned by individuals and families.

There is nothing in the world that is unknown.

From a Pohnpeian Proverb

Three Ways of Fishing on Pohnpei

Agriculture is quite important on Pohnpei. Fish, however, is a prominent part of the diet of Ponapeans and there are three main methods used on the island.

Fish hooks made from the shells of mollusks or turtle shells were formerly used and found in abundance in the area. However, these have been almost entirely replaced by imported metal hooks. Also, locally made fishing lines from coconut husk have been replaced by imported nylon lines.

Fishing with a pole and a line from the shore or the edge of the reef is widespread, although mangrove swamps cover much of the shoreline. This method requires little equipment and is simply a matter of throwing a baited hook on a line into the water. The same equipment may be used from a paddling canoe in deeper water outside of the reef.

Fishing with nets is also commmon and different nets are used. Especially important are the framed hand nets used by women. A group of neighbors wades over the fringing reef and then forms a circle around a school of fish. The circle is then closed and the fish are simply scooped up with the nets. Nets are also used by individuals at times, but with less success than when women fish in groups.

A method of catching fish with spears has been practiced on Pohnpei for a very long time. Wooden fishing spears, some with multiple points made from coral or shells, were formerly common throughout the area. Now, however, small metal spears, often propelled by a strip of the innertube of a tire, have largely replaced other types of spears. Spear fishing can be done both day and night by men, women, and children. Illumination is necessary at night to attract the fish, and this is done with a large light or with dry palm frond torches.

In the past, Pohnpeians had to rely on locally made paddle or sailing outrigger canoes to fish in the lagoon and beyond the reef. Today, larger dories are constructed and gasoline fueled engines make more areas accessible for fishing.

A great variety of sea food is found in the lagoon and beyond the reef. These include turtle, tuna, eel and shark. The techniques used in fishing are not necessarily the same on all of the islands in the state. In general, the people who live on the atolls, especially Kapingamarangi and Nukuoro in the south, are better fishermen than the high islanders. They must rely more on fish for their diet than Pohnpeians do.

Fish is probably the most common food eaten on Pohnpei. Deep line fishing for tuna beyond the reef is practiced, and also trolling. However, the methods used by most Pohnpeians are pole-fishing, net-fishing, and spear-fishing.

There is no sense following an escaped fish.

From a Pohnpeian Proverb

Traditional and Present Funeral Practices on Pohnpei

Funerals on Pohnpei combine modern practices with traditional rites. Also, a funeral is not just a family matter as all people in the community take part in the mourning.

When a person dies, the family of the deceased will notify the *Soumas*, the leader of the community. The Soumas, or his representatives, will then contact the chief of the municipality, the *Nahnmwarki*, for permission to bury the body and to ask him to attend the funeral. This will not be done ordinarily, however. Instead, the Soumas will bring two stalks of sugarcane. If one is presented, only permission to bury the body is requested. If both are present, attendance at the funeral is requested as well. In communicating with this symbol of death, the Soumas will hold the stalk of the cane with its leaves pointed toward the Nahnmwarki. When only asking permission for burial, the Nahnmwarki immediately accepts the sugarcane, as he would not refuse this. At times and for various reasons he might not be able to attend the funeral, however. The Nahnmwarki would then appoint a representative to attend the funeral in his place.

It is our present custom to visit the deceased, bringing rice, biscuits, coffee, canned meat, and other imported items. These will be given to the family and served during mourning. At the coffin, there is always a lady awaiting the new arrivals. When a visitor approaches, she will cry and wail as the visitors join her. After enough people have gathered, the men will begin pounding the root of the sakau plant to make the local drink, while the women begin cooking to feed the mourners. Those not involved will simply sit quietly. At nightfall, a group of men and women place themselves by the coffin and sing and pray. Since guests continue to arrive, the cooking never ceases and the drinking of sakau is also continued.

At daybreak, most of the men, especially the relatives of the deceased, will return to their homes to gather yams, pigs, dogs, and breadfruit, with which to complete the *uhmw*, or food, in a stone oven. The uhmw is a most important event at funeral ceremonies. When the Nahnmwarki arrives and assumes his place in the *nahs*, or house, a special sakau is brought before him and pounded. The first drink is offered to the Nahnmwarki. After he drinks, other guests can then join in the drinking.

After all of the relatives have arrived, they are then notified to give their farewell to the dead. At this time, the ladies cry very loudly, but, as in most places, the men do not cry in public. However, some are so overcome with grief that they do. The coffin is then closed and taken to the grave while a large crowd precedes and follows it.

After arrival at the burial site, the coffin is lowered into the ground. At this time, every person present picks up a piece of earth or a small stone or branch and throws it into the grave with the coffin while a choir sings the hymn of death. Everyone then returns to the home of the deceased.

Back at the nahs, the sakau plant is again brought before the Nahnmwarki and all of the branches are removed except for one, which is put aside for him. By this time, the uhmw is also ready. A quantity of food is set aside for the Nahnmwarki, and other high titled people are served. Then the rest of the food is served to others present. After this, anyone wishing to leave may do so, but the family will remain together and prepare another uhmw the next day.

During the fourth day following the death, some men will go fishing and some will remain behind to prepare food. When the fishermen return, one of them will be chosen to place part of the catch on the grave and the remainder of the fish will be brought to members of the family. When the fishermen arrive they will be rubbed with coconut oil and given wreaths of flowers, *mwaramwars*, and also served sakau. Seven days or more after the death, the remainder of the food left over from the funeral will be served.

Since Pohnpei's population is large and contains a number of groups of people, there are some variations in the funeral customs that are followed. The practices mentioned above, however, are those followed by most people on the island, from my experience.

Sharpening a knife before going to a funeral is bad luck.

Pohnpeian Belief

Pohnpeian Shell Horn, "*sewi*"

Pohnpei State Outliers

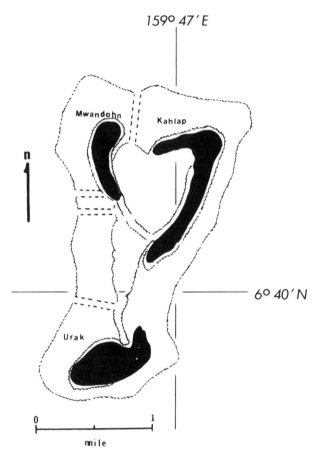

159° 47′ E

6° 40′ N

0 _____ 1
mile

Mokil

Land area: 0.48 square mile
Population: 289 in 73 households
Main Cultural Group: Eastern Carolinians
Main Language: Mokilese (Ponapean)
Population Center: Kahlap
Political: a municipality of Ponape State of the F.S.M.

A man should not feel bad when turned down by a girl, because it happens to every man at some time.

From a Mokilese Proverb

Childbirth Customs on Mokil

Childbirth is an important occasion on Mokil, and so celebrations and ceremonies associated with it are taken quite seriously. Down through the years they have changed very little.

It is the custom that when a woman is pregnant with her first child, both sides of her immediate family must care for her and prevent her from doing any hard work. During her late months of pregnancy, a small feast will be held for her by members of both her and her husband's families. The ceremony, called *sou*, which means clan on Mokil, takes place during her eighth month of pregnancy. At this time, chants are said that will bring luck for a healthy mother and baby. Clanship on Mokil is passed through the mother to the child. Whether it survives the birth or not, it is already a member of the clan of the mother, and so will be all other children that come afterwards.

At the time of delivery, only women are allowed to assist the midwife, and usually her aunts or other female relatives will be present. No one from the husband's side is allowed to see her at this time. However, after the baby is born and has been cleaned, her husband should be the first to see it. It is his responsibility to take the placenta and bury it. By doing this, it is believed that the child will always pay attention to the father's commands and obey his wishes.

Most customs after a birth apply to all babies and not only to the first-born. Ten days after the birth, a celebration will take place. On this occasion, only members of the two immediate families should contribute and participate. For a first-born, however, everyone is invited to attend. The purpose of this feast is to show off the new member of the family. It also offers an opportunity for people to show their material wealth by their contribution.

Following childbirth, the new mother receives special care and must remain at her home. Foods will be provided regularly to enrich the milk in her breast, and she might remain at her house for as long as five months. During this time, it is customary for relatives to visit the new baby and bring gifts of food or other items. Failure to bring a gift is considered shameful and the person who visited empty-handed would be looked down upon. Cousins in the extended family and close friends will spend the first ten nights with the newly born's family.

The largest celebration usually takes place when the child is a year old, or it might be earlier or later as the father decides on the time. Although everyone is allowed to join in this feast, the responsibility for it rests on the father's side of the family. The most important food served at this time is pig, but taro, bread-fruit, preserved breadfruit, and other local foods are also popular. Distribution of local oil is an important part of this occasion and the oil is provided by the woman's family. All of the female elders attending are given a bottle of coconut oil by the new mother.

Ceremonies and celebrations remain the same even if the new mother is unmarried. To the people of Mokil, the baby is more important than the woman. Her father would assume the responsibilities that would normally be her husband's, however.

If the woman marries later and has a child, and this child is the first-born for her husband, all of the ceremonies and celebrations for a first-born will take place again.

Most customs on Mokil are still practiced, with slight changes from the past. Instead of giving local oil, imported perfumes might be distributed. In the past, the naming of the child was done by the grandparents of the father, but this is not necessarily true any longer. What has not changed at all is that childbirth remains the most important occasion in a new couple's life.

A black raven flying over a house means a member of the family is pregnant.

Molilese Belief

History of Land Ownership on Mokil

Land ownership on Mokil is complicated by cultural considerations and foreign administrations. However, as on all islands in Micronesia, ownership of land is of great importance on the island.

Before the great typhoon of 1770, there was probably no private ownership of land. Very little taro seems to have been grown at that time, but the products of the land were probably freely available to everyone. The large taro patch on the islet of Kalap was under the sea and the only wet taro was grown on a comparatively small patch on Urak Islet. The important taro patch on Kalap was reclaimed from the sea by filling in the channel after the typhoon.

There were few people remaining on the island after this natural disaster. As the population increased, however, the families had to decide how to distribute the land. Finally, it was decided to divide the land among the families on Kalap, as this was the only inhabited islet until around 1850. (Later, people moved to the islet of Mwandon to be near the visiting whaling ships. When the whalers stopped coming, however, everyone returned to Kalap.)

In 1852, a visit to Mokil was made by a certian N.J. Anderson, who said that the population numbered about 87 at that time. According to Anderson, Americans had arrived that same year and dominated the land by establishing themselves as lords. They supplied whalers with pigs, chickens and vegetables and were making much money. The Mokilese were receiving only a little cloth, tobacco, and gin.

The typhoon of 1905, while probably not as disastrous as the pre-historic one of 1770 was, nevertheless, devastating to the land. Starvation would have taken place had the German administration on Ponape not sent relief and temporarily moved part of the population to Ponape. The Germans estimate that half of the coconut trees were destroyed and almost all provisions were lost.

During the German administraton, the land was deeded to individuals. As it happened, applications had to be filed and this was a process which few people understood. As a result, the land was distributed unequally and those working for the church had an advantage in obtaining titles to the land.

At present, the three islets of Mokil are divided into many sections and they have names to identify parts of the islets. These sections in turn are sub-divided by ownership and rapid population growth has caused many divisions. Whereas inheritance of land at one time was simple, and the land went to the oldest son, today it is much more complicated. Land is often divided equally among all children in a family. Also, a daughter might be given land to bring to the family of her husband.

Small bait, small fish. Big bait, big fish.

From a Mokilese Proverb

Marriage Customs in the Past on Mokil

It is not certain how marriages originated on Mokil. We do know, however, that marriages took place long before there was any contact with the outside world. But as far as can be remembered, no wedding ceremonies, as we know them today, existed on the island until the arrival of the missionaries in the last century.

In the old days, when a marriage was desired, the boy's parents would visit those of the girl and discuss the proposal. The boy might or might not accompany them on this occasion. If both sets of parents agreed on the marriage, the girl would be brought in and questioned. If her responses were acceptable, she would then be taken by the boy's parents to their home. From then on, they were considered to be married.

Before the arrival of the missionaries on Mokil, polygamy was occasionally practiced. One way for a man to acquire a second wife was to defeat an opponent in battle. The man who won would take not only his opponent's property, but also his wife.

Although the decision of parents in marriage is very important today, it was far more important in the past on Mokil. When a boy became skilled in canoe building, house construction, and could dig a small taro patch with other men, the parents would consider their son to be ready for marriage. They would then make the arrangements with a girl's parents. The boy and the girl were seldom in love. They probably knew each other only because the island was so small, but it was unlikely that they ever talked about marriage. Whether they liked each other or not, they would abide by the decision of their parents. This custom continues today, although it is not as strong as in the past.

Another characteristic of Mokilese marriage that was more prominent in the past than today was selecting a partner from within the same extended family. Since land is often given as a dowry in marriage, this custom insured that the land remained within the same family.

Today, marriage on Mokil is like that of many other islands in Micronesia. Once wedding plans are agreed upon by the parents, both families will gather and prepare food, and friends will assist in preparing it. Everyone will attend a Protestant wedding ceremony in a church. Then a marriage feast will follow. After the feast, the couple will stay with the man's parents and take care of them. However, if the parents of the bride have no other children, the couple will reside with her family.

If a woman takes another woman's husband, another woman will come along and take the man away from her.

From a Mokilese Proverb

How the Islets of Mokil
Were Formed and Named

The atoll of Mokil has three islets with unusual names and different characteristics. Three brothers long ago were responsible for these different characteristics, and for finding and naming the islets. Also, the three brothers and their mother were responsible for the coconut palm trees so prevalent on Mokil today.

The three brothers were named Ur, Mwa, and Ka. Ur was the first-born son, Mwa was the next born, and Ka was the youngest. When these three boys were growing up their parents provided everything for them. The boys were also taught very practical skills by their mother and father. They were trained to dig and plant taro in patches, to climb trees in order to collect coconuts and breadfruit, and to build fine canoes. They also learned how to fish. The three boys were not equally good in all of these skills, however. Although Ur and Mwa could grow crops to support themselves, they were not the best farmers. Ka was the best farmer, but the poorest fisherman of the three.

When they all went fishing together, Ka, the youngest, had difficulty catching fish for himself. His brothers laughed and made fun of him because they were better fishermen. Sometimes Ka would ask his older brothers to let him use their fish hooks, but this only made them laugh more. Only when the older brothers had a bad hook would they give it to Ka. When he used the hook, it would tangle on a rock continually, and Ur and Mwa would laugh even more.

On one particular day all of the brothers went fishing together in the same canoe. The hook of Ka again got tangled and others laughed as usual and teased him. Ka then pulled hard, but the hook would not budge. Then the younger brother pulled and tugged as hard as he possibly could. When he felt something move, all of the brothers realized that an unusual occurrence was happening. Ka kept pulling his fishing line even harder. At last, an island was pulled to the surface, and it consisted of three islets.

The three brothers were very happy at this unusual surprise. Ur and Mwa began to call it ''our'' island, but Ka told them that it was not ''our'' island, but ''his'' island, and he would decide what to do with it. He said that he would give his brothers none of the land unless they told him their secrets of fishing. Since both Ur and Mwa wanted land very badly, they agreed to part with their secrets. Ka then learned to fish as well as his brothers.

Since it was Ka who pulled up the islets, he had the right to decide what should be done with them. To Ur, because he was older and a good fisherman, he gave the largest islet with the best fishing area. Ka kept for himself the second largest islet because it had good land for farming and gardening. The other islet was given to Mwa because it also had a good fishing area. The three brothers named the islets after themselves, and these islets have these names to this day. The oldest brother, Ur, called his Urak; the youngest brother, Ka, named his Kahlap, and the smallest islet was named by Mwa, Mwandohn.

The mother of the three brothers was very much loved by them, but time passed, and she eventually died. After she was buried, a coconut tree grew up from her grave. Its first fruit was a dry, immature nut which had three corners, and so the boys named the corners of the nut after themselves in the order of their ages: Ur, Mwa, Ka. This was their valuable heritage from their mother. The tree produced many, many more nuts and these were planted on the three islets of Mokil. Because of the brothers, the Mokilese word for a young coconut is *urmwaka*.

There is evidence on Mokil today that this story is true. Coconut trees, the mother's gift from her grave, abound on all three islets. The largest taro patch is found today on Kahlap because Ka was the best farmer and the best fishing areas are found off Urak and Mwahdohn because of the fishing skills of Ur and Mwa. Also, one can see today the line used by Ka to raise the islets in the form of a reef dividing the lagoon into two parts.

Two coconuts hitting the ground at the same time means that a ship will soon arrive.

Mokilese Belief

Activities Before and After a Death
on Mokil

Mokil Atoll has three small islets so news of a death spreads rapidly by word of mouth.

When a person dies, a senior male member of the deceased's family will take charge of delegating responsibilities for the funeral. The deceased will be dressed in his best clothes and all of the people on the island will come together to bid farewell to the body. Songs will be sung and prayers will be offered throughout the first night after the death. A person is never buried immediately after dying on Mokil. Burial will follow the next day. The family of the deceased will prepare food for the guests who arrive. From early evening until about midnight, children will sing songs. After that, the adults will continue singing until dawn.

On the day following the death, the body is taken to a church before burial. Since the Protestant religion is the only one on Mokil, a Protestant ceremony is held. There is no communal burial ground on the island, and each family has its own cemetery. Before the body is lowered into the grave, another final service is held.

Following the burial, the grave will be decorated by the family of the deceased. The young girls of the island will help in this by removing old decorations and replacing them every other day. The main decoration is flowers. On the 40th day after the funeral, the last decoration will be put on the grave.

After a death, adults and children of the island will come and stay with the family of the deceased. This always helps to ease the sorrow of the family. Adults will offer prayers every morning and evening until the 40th day.

On Mokil, ceremonies for a child or an adult would be the same. Wealthy people and community leaders might have larger funerals, however, but the procedure is the same.

There are actually three ceremonies to be observed. At the first one, all of the islanders would attend and a feast would then be held. Those attending would bring food to donate, but the family would provide the most food. The second largest feast would take place 40 days after the death. On this occasion, all people are not required to attend, but only the family and those who choose to come. It is believed that the spirit of the deceased will remain with the family for 40 days. The final feast would take place one year after the date of the death. Only the family would observe this occasion, but they might choose to invite others.

Other anniversaries of a death might be observed in following years. The length of time depends on the family's love and respect for the deceased.

If a seabird cries on the roof of your house, a relative is going to die.
Molikese Belief

Pohnpeian Church Cemetery

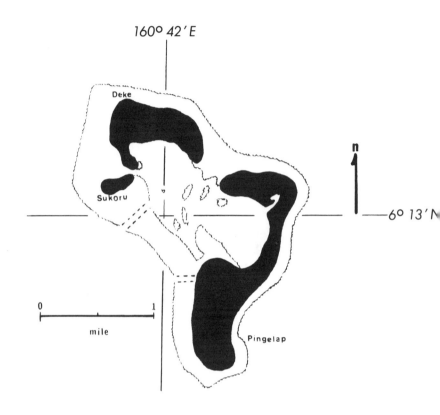

Pingelap

Land area: 0.68 square mile
Population: 369 in 70 households
Main Cultural Group: Eastern Carolinian
Main Language: Pinglapese (Pohnpeian)
Population Center: Pingelap
Political: a municipality of Pohnpei State of the F.S.M.

Weaving a mat while the husband is away fishing will cause the husband to catch no fish.

Pinglapese Belief

Present Childbirth Activities
on Pingelap

There are a number of traditional restrictions for a pregnant woman on Pingelap Atoll. All of these exist for the health of the expectant mother and her unborn baby. There are also traditional activities that follow the birth of the child.

During pregnancy, she must be served local medicine that is cooling to the stomach. She should not eat while walking nor should she sit for long periods of time. Also, she should not cut her fingernails until the day she delivers the child. The husband will always be sure that she has whatever she desires at this time. Until after her delivery, however, there will be no formal celebrations or ceremonies.

There are women on Pingelap who are specialists in caring for expectant mothers, and one of these women will be called by the family to attend to the pregnant woman. Following the delivery, friends and relatives will be notified immediately by word of mouth, and those off the island will be told of the birth by mail. Those on the island will bring gifts such as soaps, diapers, and towels for the baby. Other gifts will be healthy foods for the mother to enrich the milk in her breasts.

If the baby is the first-born child of the couple, a big feast, called *kamadipu in meseni* in Pingelapese, will be held. This celebration takes place on the eighth day following the birth and is held at the house of the new parents. On this day, the child will be named. Food is served and a minister always attends.

After childbirth, members of the family prepare large quantities of food for the mother. She is encouraged to eat as much as possible, and even to eat in the middle of the night if she is awake. The husband will always see to it that meat is prepared for his wife at this time.

Adoption is quite common on Pingelap. The baby might be adopted by its grandparents or by an aunt or an uncle. Adoption usually takes place one or two months after the birth of the baby. The couple adopting the child always takes part in the kamadipu in meseni.

On Pingelap, different people might name the child. It could be named by its real father or by the parents who adopt it. It is quite common, however, to name it after its grandfather if it is a boy or its grandmother if it is a girl.

169

Perhaps the one outstanding aspect of childbirth to a foreigner visiting Pingelap is the frequency of adoption. However, in Pingelapese society it is felt that a child belongs to all of the people and not just the natural father and mother. Also, with the small size of Pingelap, both the natural parents and the foster parents are near the child continuously.

As the father is, the son will be.

From a Pingelapese Proverb

Palm Frond Baby Basket

Foods and Eating Habits
on Pingelap

For an atoll with such a small land area as Pingelap, a surprising number of foods are grown. Naturally, however, they do not grow in abundance and much of the food comes from the sea. Of the main foods—bananas, coconuts, pandanas, sugarcane, yams, papayas, arrow-roots, taro, and breadfruit—the latter two are most commonly eaten in addition to fish.

Taro, when properly stored, can last three to four months. To preserve this food it is first boiled. The cooked taro is then cut into pieces and placed in the sun until it is very dry and hard. They are then put into sacks for storage. When the taro is needed, the pieces are put back into water until they become soft and then they are again boiled. Coconut milk is added to help this process. After boiling, they are ready to be served. Taro's main limitation is that it will only grow in muddy soil in the center of the island. Each family, however, has its own rows in the taro patch.

Breadfruit is also of great importance because it can be preserved. Unlike taro, breadfruit is stored under the ground on Pingelap and it differs from other breadfruit found on Pohnpei. The variety found on Pingelap is small and contains many seeds in the dough that make it difficult to store. First, the skin is removed and the fruit is cut into four pieces. They are then placed in salt water overnight so that it will be easier to separate the seeds from the fruit. When the seeds have been removed, the fruit is stored in a hole in the ground that is lined with the leaves of the breadfruit tree. When the preserved breadfruit is needed, the hole is uncovered and the dough is removed and boiled. It can then be served with or without coconut milk. This is quite popular food at feasts on the island.

Pingelapese do not consider eating with utensils to be important, especially at feasts. People eat together in groups with banana leaves for plates and coconut shells for cups. Families might eat together or some members might eat separately. Those who are farming usually eat only twice each day while children remaining at home might eat four or five times daily. It is not necessary for the father and older sons to eat before going to work, as the work must come first. When a family eats together, the food is served first to the father, and then down the line to the youngest child and the mother.

Taro and breadfruit, along with fish, of course, remain the staple foods on the island. Being able to preserve them allows Pingelapese to eat them all year round. Once each year, farmers will exhibit the largest taro they have grown in their patches and the winner will receive local prestige on the island.

The first fish that bites when you are fishing must be caught, otherwise you will have bad luck fishing.

Pingelapese Belief

Why the Islets of Pingelap
are Separated

A stretch of lagoon sits between the islets of Dedi and Sukoru on Pingelap Atoll at present. At one time, however, these islets were a single piece of land. They became separated when a god from the Marshall Islands visited the atoll and caused the lagoon to form.

On the western side of Jaluit Atoll in the Marshalls, at an area sticking out from the rest of the land, sits an islet named Pingelap.

A stretch of lagoon sits between the islets of Deke and Sukoru where a god took sand from Pingelap in Pohnpei State and deposited it at Jaluit.

Long ago the people of Pingelap worshipped a god named Isopaw. He was a lazy god and his greatest pleasure was sleeping away the days. He would only awaken briefly at night. On a day while Isopaw was sleeping, another god from Jaluit appeared on Deke. He was careful not to awaken Isopaw, and he took a gigantic handfull of sand from the area causing a trench to form that became a lagoon between Deke and Sukoru. The people watched this unusual happening, and then they immediately awakened Isopaw and told him the news. Isopaw asked in what direction the other god had gone, and was told that it was directly to the east. Isopaw then hurried after the strange god.

By the time that Isopaw caught up with the other god, they had traveled all the way to Jaluit. When the Marshallese god saw Isopaw, he dropped all of the sand that he was carrying and hurried away. The sand was spread over such a large area of the reef that Isopaw could not hope to pick it all up, so he left it all on Jaluit and returned to Pingelap.

From that time onward, a lagoon has separated Deke from Sukoru. This is at the exact place where the Marshallese god scooped up the sand while Isopaw slept. Also, there is an islet on Jaluit that is named after the incident, "Pingelap," and this is where the god dropped the sand when being chased by Isopaw.

Big talkers, small doers.

From a Pingelapese Proverb

Past and Present Religion on Pingelap

Information about the early religious practices on Pingelap before the arrival of Christianity has been passed by word of mouth from ancestors of those living on the island today. According to the stories, the only religion of the early Pingelapese was animalism, and five gods were worshipped. However, each god was worshipped differently, in a different place, and at a different time of the year. Leaders on the island were selected to conduct services for each god.

The gods had an order of supremacy. The overall god was Isopau, and the leader selected to conduct services was *Dokasa*, or king. Other leaders might conduct services for Isopau, but only upon the king's request. He was worshipped at Mweniap. The next god was Rarori, and the assigned leader for the services was *Nanawa*, or *Wasahi*, the second highest ranking man. Services were held at Perku. The god Lisokosok had Nanpas to hold services at Ilong and the god Nawilap's servies were held at Mweimok by Nalaimw. (Mweimok is known at Pelenekeus today.) The final god, Naliolopwong, had the distinction that all leaders were responsible for conducting services for him, usually at Sukoro. Naliolopwong was the only god not living on Meseirong, the main island of Pingelap Atoll.

In 1872, Christianity was introduced and worship of the traditional gods began to decline. In that year, a group of Pingelapese who had been working at the Protestant mission on Pohnpei under Reverend Tom of Boston returned home. Some of their names have been forgotten, but three of these young men are still remembered well for the work that they accomplished. Thomas is remembered as the leader of the group, and others were David and Robert. (Robert, incidentally, was the grandfather of the late Elias Robert, a former Deputy Director of the Community College of Micronesia on Pohnpei.) In the group were members of respected families, and this helped them considerably in setting up the Protestant religion.

The group of Pingelapese missionaries first sought the attention of the king and told him what they were attempting to do. They impressed the king so much that he decided to join them, and he called on other leaders to do likewise. As the people saw their leaders become Christians, they stopped worshipping their traditional gods and also joined the church. Today, people believe that the coming of Christianity caused the traditional gods to leave Pingelap.

From that time onward, the Protestant church has been the only religion on the island. In about 1892, a Pingelapese named Andon, who had attended Ohwa Christian Training School on Pohnpei, returned and attempted to establish the Roman Catholic religion, but he failed. In 1971, there were representatives of other religions sent to the island but they also failed. Today, the Congregational denomination of the Protestant church remains the only one in Pingelap.

Sneezing four times in a row means that lots of rain is coming.
Pingelapese Belief

Boat Construction on Pingelap

There are few vehicles on Pingelap Atoll. Most transportation consists of using one's legs along trails, or boats to travel between the three islets of the atoll. Boat construction, then, has always been important to Pingelapese.

In the last century, before the Japanese administration, building good boats was not common, and it was not until after 1914 that boat construction showed great improvement. Design of boats was improved by competition. Pingelap was divided into four sections, and each section would make a boat of its own. After this, each section would have a party to celebrate the completion of the task. Then a competition would be held to determine which section had built the fastest and most seaworthy craft. The best boat would then be the model for the future boat construction.

When Pingelapese began building boats for individuals, the same cooperation took place as when a section of the island built a boat. For instance, if a man in one section desired a boat for himself, other men would immediately offer their help. However, there would be no payment offered or expected for the labor. The only thing necessary is that the man who will own the boat provide food for the workers to eat during the day while working.

During the Japanese times, local materials for boat building were used much more than they are today. These include lumber from the breadfruit tree for the hull, while the keel was made from other hard woods such as *pene* and *ikoik*. Limbs from the hibiscus tree were used for the ribs of boats. The only things imported at the time were nails, putty, and paints.

A disadvantage, or perhaps an advantage, to boat building on Pingelap is that much time must be taken in construction. There is no sawmill to prepare lumber and so each piece of the boat must be worked by hand. Preparing the lumber might take a month and sometimes two. Two or three additional weeks are also needed to put the prepared pieces together. Just fashioning the ribs might take a full week. However, in preparing pieces by hand, a lot of good craftsmanship goes into the final product, and it is likely that a Pingelapese handmade boat will last as long as one made with machine-prepared wooden parts.

Each person has his own personal ways or skills with which to accomplish tasks.

From a Pingelapese Proverb

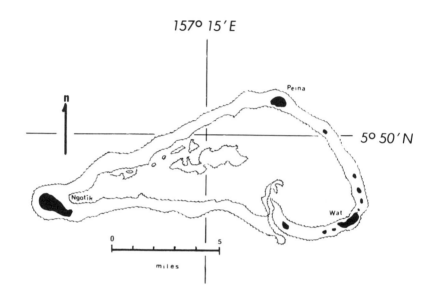

Ngatik

Land area: 0.67 square mile
Population: 567 in 86 households
Main Cultural Group: Eastern Carolinian
Main Language: Ngatikese (Pohnpeian)
Population Center: Ngatik
Political: a municipality of Pohnpei State of the F.S.M.

The reef of Ngatik is very long. There is plenty of time to do things in life.
From a Ngatikese Proverb

Land Ownership on Ngatik

To Ngatikese, land ownership is of great importance and land is probably the most valued possession. Land containing soil where taro will grow is especially desired.

Land on the island that belongs to a family is shared by all members, and each has equal rights to its use. In caring for the property, the father acts as the overseer, however. It is his responsibility to watch the condition of the land and determine if it has been overused and also to see that all those wishing to use it may do so. Although land is shared by all in a family, the father's permission should always be sought when using it. When he is not available, the mother assumes this role.

When a father dies, the usual custom is for the land to be divided equally among the children. There are exceptions to this, however. If a father happens to have left a will that has been witnessed, the property will be divided according to the father's wishes. Most often on Ngatik, when a father dies without distributing his land or leaving a will, the children will choose to continue to share the land equally. This only works effectively, though, if they can share without quarreling.

On a number of islands in Pohnpei State, land ownership dates back to the German administration. On such islands as Pohnpei, the Germans issued deeds to show ownership of a piece of land. This did not happen on Ngatik, however, because the Germans did not issue certificates on the island. In fact, all of the outer islands were less under foreign influence thatn Pohnpei. A plan for land distribution did develop, however. This plan provided for a committee of seven members, the Isimen. One of its main responsiblities was to set boundaries and landmarks to show land belonging to a particular family. The committee functioned well and was in existence until it was replaced by municipal officials called councilmen.

At present, rights to inherit land still follow the parent-children custom that is traditional on Ngatik. This is not written law, however. Disputes over ownership do occur and a legal decision is the last thing that Ngatikese like to resort to. First, there will be attempts to settle disputes by the individuals concerned and councilmen might be asked to help. Also, some other highly respected members of the community will be asked for their opinions. In most instances, the matter will be settled and will go no further, but when all else fails, the case is subject to Pohnpei state law, and a court would make the final decision of legal ownership.

A man should eat like the Peluhs bird, sparingly and not stuff his stomach. He eats a little, flies away, and then eats a little again.

From a Pohnpeian Proverb

House Construction on Ngatik

Two types of houses are found on Ngatik Atoll and these might loosely be called traditional and modern styles. The traditional style is by far the most common and is made almost entirely of materials found on the island that are available at no cost. Although a modern style home requires imported materials, some things used, such as sand and gravel for a concrete floor, are found in abundance on Ngatik. Despite the use of different materials for each style, the procedure and spirit of cooperation of people are the same in building them.

When a local house is being built, all of the relatives and neighbors will gather to help. The women will divide into groups and some will be preparing thatch for the roof while other make rope from coconut trees that will be used to fasten the thatch to poles. Meanwhile, the men will be cutting various lengths of poles from strong trees for the frame of the house.

When the construction begins, the main support pillars will first be put in place. Then the skeleton, or frame, will be completed. This heavy work might take all day, and on the following day the roof will be put on. This is interesting to watch since no nails are used to attach the thatch. Instead, locally woven rope is used. The men use a small stick, slightly thicker than a pencil, called a *kohr* to work with. The rope is put around the stick and inserted through the thatch and then fastened to the roof on sticks. As some men work on the roof, others are standing below to hand up the thatch that has been prepared by the women. It could take all morning to complete this, depending on the size of the roof and the number of workers who are available.

The floor construction is the next project. Floors in Ngatikese houses are usually built two or three feet above the ground. Boards made of breadfruit and other large trees are used, but sometimes floors are made from bamboo.

The final construction is the walls. Some people use tin, or imported boards from a sawmill, but these are expensive items. Thatch is more commonly used. Since Ngatakese prefer open air houses, the walls are usually made only half way up the frame of the house. When the day's work has been done, the women will prepare food for the workers.

Traditional houses do not last as long as modern style houses, but they are often more comfortable to live in. Also, this island has plenty of pandanus and coconut leaves for roofs and walls and strong woods for house frames. The labor is volunteered, and so the price of a brand new traditional house on Ngatik is usually nothing.

Planting a sharp stick outside of one's house will help to chase away evil spirits.

Pohnpeian Belief

Death and Burial on Ngatik

All of the people of Ngatik are affected when a death occurs on the island. It is a time of mourning by the entire community, and grief is expressed before, during, and after the actual burial.

When a person dies, every member of the extended family of the deceased will rush to his home. When they have gathered together, the women will dress and prepare the body for burial while men construct a coffin. As soon as the coffin is finished, the body will immediately be placed in it. At this time, the women will sit around the coffin and express their grief by crying.

Before the burial, all of the people on the island may visit the body. The religious leader will also visit to pray for the dead. They

179

will sing hymns and do whatever possible to help the family. Some speeches telling of the merits of the deceased are always given at this time to comfort the family. Songs will be sung throughout the night and the family of the deceased will prepare food and drink for those singing, as well as for other guests who remain awake throughout the night.

On the day following the death, the body will be carried to its place of burial and a short service will be held. A religious leader will once again offer prayers for the dead. The grave will have been dug before the arrival of the coffin. Finally, when the coffin is lowered into the grave, those attending will throw stones or a handful of dirt into the grave. At this time, all of the women present will cry louder and louder to express their grief. After the burial has been completed, the head of the family of the deceased will appoint a member to express the appreciation that they feel for the cooperation of those attending the funeral.

It is usually during the day following the funeral that a large feast is held. This occasion is organized by the family of the deceased as a tribute to the one who has died and as a way of showing appreciation to those who have assisted them. All of the people on Ngatik will usually attend this feast. The public will also bring various foods and give them to the family in order to help them feed the many guests. Popular foods at this time are pork and taro, and it would be quite unusual for a guest to arrive without a gift of food for the occasion.

After the feast, relatives will remain with the family for varying lengths of time and unrelated guests will return to their homes. Three days after the burial, the grave will be visited by the family and new decorations will be placed on it. There is no official period of mourning on Ngatik and this would conclude the ceremonies for the dead.

A star appearing very close to the moon is a sign of death.
Pohnpeian Belief

Catholic Church Ruins, Pohnpei

181

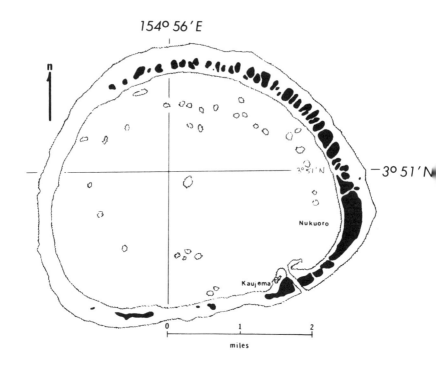

154° 56' E

3° 51' N

Nukuoro

Kaujema

miles

Nukuoro

Land area: 0.64 square mile
Population: 308 in 73 households
Main Cultural Group: Polynesians
Main Lanugage: Nukuoran (Polynesian)
Population Center: Nukuoro
Political: a municipality of Pohnpei State of the F.S.M.

No man vomits up something, and then swallows it down again. Be careful what you say so that you don't have to swallow words after saying them.

From a Pohnpeian Proverb

Structures and Building on Nukuoro

Nukuoro has the distinction of being one of the only two Polynesian Islands in Micronesia. Since it is quite isolated from normal trade routes, local, rather than imported, materials are used in construction of most houses.

The atoll is close to the equator and the temperature usually varies from eighty to ninety degrees. As a result, the people live mostly in thatched roof houses that allow for the circulation of air. Local materials are preferred because imported materials are quite expensive.

A typical Nukuoro settlement would have the sleeping house some distance from the beach to afford protection from the strong winds. The cooking houses would be close by. Toilets, however, are never built on land and are found over the shallow water. The canoe houses would be very close to the beach. Canoes, incidentally, are the only means of transportation used on Nukuoro other than walking.

The main material for roofing is one of two kinds of thatch. One is obtained from dead coconut fronds that are woven together in a way so that rain will not penetrate.

In building a sleeping house for a single person, about 300 of these thatches are needed. Coconut thatch will only last for one or two years on a roof, and so another type is obtainable from the pandanus tree. These are collected and attached to a stick. A pandanus thatch roof might last as long as ten years.

The actual building of a thatch roofed house takes a lot of time and effort. In addition to about ten men who will be asked to help, the builder will also invite women and girls to weave the thatch. Wood is obtained from trees on the island and a locally made string is used in place of nails. The floor is covered with gravel and sand from the beach. The walls are made from sticks with spaces between them that allow a breeze to pass through the house. Woven mats are attached as walls and these can be lowered when privacy is desired.

Houses built long ago were much stronger than those of today, and it is said on Nukuoro that the old houses could withstand even a coconut tree falling on them. It seems that stronger materials were used and more time was taken in building a house in the past.

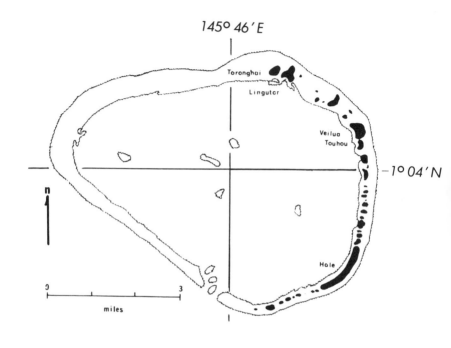

145° 46' E

Toronghai
Lingutar
Veilua
Touhou
-1° 04' N
n
Hole
0
3
miles

Kapingamarangi

Land area: 0.52 square mile
Population: 510 in 111 households
Main Cultural Group: Polynesian
Main Lanugage: Kapingamarangan (Polynesian)
Population Centers: Touhou, Vielua
Political: a municipality of Ponape State of the F.S.M.

Pointing with your fingers at birds following a school of fish will cause the fishermen to catch no fish.

Kapingamarangan Belief

184

Traditional Childbirth Customs
on Kapingamarangi

There are no celebrations or ceremonies before childbirth on Kapingamarangi. In the past, however, there was a certain procedure that had to be followed by all expectant mothers.

When a woman reached about her sixth month of pregnancy, she would be required to rest, do no work, and walk around as little as possible. She would leave the home of her husband and move into the house of the chief where women would provide food and care for her. Her parents would also provide the proper foods for their daughter, although they would not live with her. At this time, the woman would not pay any attention to her physical appearance and would not even comb her hair. Her husband would also neglect his appearance, let his hair grow, and would not even bathe. In this way, he had a look of sadness. This was in preparation for sorrow in the event that the mother or child did not survive the delivery. Special talented women were available during the late months of pregnancy to massage the stomach area of the pregnant woman. This was done so that the unborn baby would be in the correct position for delivery. Massaging is still common today on Kapingamarangi. A midwife would reside with the expectant mother until it was time for delivery. When the woman went into labor, she would be taken by the midwife and her female relatives to shallow water in the ocean. Here she would lie down and be held by the arms by either one or two women. Babies were then delivered in the shallow water of the sea. After the umbilical cord was separated, it would be buried in a special symbolic place. If the baby was female it wold be buried under a beautiful flowering tiger lily plant; for a male child it would be buried beside a young coconut tree.

Following the delivery, the midwife would appoint a woman to tell other women in the community about the birth. The women would then gather together, form a procession, and walk to the house of the chief, while saying special chants.

Several days after the birth, a ceremony took place to honor the mother and child. This occasion was held in a meeting hall that contains the tomb of Rova, wife of Utamatua, the first man on Kapingamarangi. Four to six women would form a semi-circle and chant throughout the day while the mother and infant sat near the tomb. The higher the rank of the mother, the closer to the tomb she was permitted to sit.

After delivering, the mother would remain at the house of the chief where women gave her special care. It would be the chief's decision when she was allowed to return to her husband, and this would usually be four or five months after the baby was born.

In the past, children were not named until they were ten or twelve years old and had developed particular skills. Until that time they were simply called *Tama*, meaning child. They were then usually named after the skill that they were proficient in, such as fishing, construction, weaving, or boat building.

There have been changes over the years in childbirth procedures on the atoll. Often parties are now held after the baptism of a child. However, there are still people alive today on Kapingamarangi who were born by the procedures of the past.

Wearing flowers will bring bad luck to a pregnant woman.

Pohnpeian Belief

Traditional Marriage on Kapingamarangi

Past marriage customs of the people on Kapingamarangi have been passed on by word of mouth to the present generation. Because of our Polynesian origin, our customs were probably somewhat different from those of other areas of Micronesia. What follows are the traditional marriage customs as they have been told to me. Years ago, the practices of courtship and marriage were done in a certain way. The entire purpose of courtship was to establish a marriage between a young man and a young woman.

In the first place, it was the young man who noticed the girl he wanted for his wife and initiated the contact. He would go to her home at night, awaken her and talk to her. Finally, he would ask her to become his partner. If she agreed to consider this, the period of courtship began. This was the time known as the "persuasion period" for the young man and young woman, and the man tried his best to convince the girl she should marry him. After a number of secret meetings, usually at night, the young man would take the young woman to the home of his parents. This, too, would be done at night. He would tell them that the girl has

186

agreed to marry him. The young man's mother would then prepare a place for the couple to sleep together. After they were alone, they would rarely speak to each other, because they would be very much uncertain and ashamed. On the following morning, it was usually the mother of the young man who would go to visit the parents of the young woman to discuss plans for the marriage. By this time, the girl would have returned to her home and she would not be allowed to meet her future husband again until the day of the marriage ceremony.

The celebration of the marriage was characterized by a very large wedding feast. The foods for the feast were prepared separately by the families of the young man and the young woman. The food would then be brought together and exchanged between the families. However, food for the newly married couple would be prepared by both families and would not be mixed or exchanged with the rest of the food at the feast. All members of the extended families would be involved in the wedding ceremony and would receive equal shares of food.

Before marriage, it was the responsibility of a young man's father to prepare him for the duties of being a husband. This was mainly concerned with skills of boat building, house construction, and especially fishing. The girls would be taught by their mothers in weaving, cooking, and housekeeping.

Some of the traditional customs of marriage on Kapingamarangi have been adjusted over past years, but industriousness by both a young man and a young woman is still considered to be a prime quality in marriage.

We will not lie in only one grave. A man and his wife should not be jealous of each other since they have different bodies and will be separated at death.
From a Pohnpeian Proverb

Weaving on Kapingamarangi

The people of Kapingamarangi are known throughout Micronesia for their skill in weaving. A story is told on the atoll about how the people learned this skill.

Long ago, there were no people on Kapingamarangi who knew how to weave. The story is told of a woman from Tarawa, in the Gilbert Islands, who landed on the island. She had jumped into a canoe and paddled away to escape from her husband. Luckily, she found Kapingamarangi. When she landed, she thought the islets were uninhabited but soon discovered many people there using only breadfruit leaves for their clothes. The Tarawa woman immediately began to teach the people to weave their *lava-lavas* from local materials. She then taught them to weave things used in the home, such as baskets and mats. This skill has been passed from generation to generation and today the people of Kapingamarangi are expert weavers.

Different weaving is done by different age groups. The older women only weave thatch for housing, mats, and sometimes baskets. Small items such as trays, purses, and other handicraft are made by younger women as steady hands and good eyesight are necessary.

The atoll is too small to support all of the Kapingamarangi people, and so one group stays on the island while another lives in Porakiet on Pohnpei. Both groups weave things but the group on Pohnpei does not have all of the proper materials and must get them from relatives on Kapingamarangi. The group on the atoll does the most expert weaving and even children in elementary school can often weave better than adults in Porakiet. Only a few of the group on Pohnpei actually have this weaving skill, while on Kapingamarangi, all women and young girls know how to weave.

Years ago, the articles that were woven were only those that could be used by the people. Today, however, many articles are made to be sold in craft shops to tourists visiting Pohnpei. Actually, a woman who spends all of her time weaving can earn more money than one who has a job. Popular items that are sold include trays of different colors, purses, hairpins woven with shells, fans, mats and baby cradles. Artificial flowers are also woven.

It does not take too long for an expert woman to weave something. A mat measuring seven feet by twelve feet can be made in two days. A fine, large tray can be completed in only three days if the woman has nothing else to do, and small handicrafts, such as hairpins and place mats, can be woven in less than one day.

Kapingamarangi is one of the smallest atolls in Micronesia. It is also distinctive because of the Polynesian origin of the people. However, the weaving of the women and girls has been most responsible for making Kapingamarangi famous.

When you are in the water fishing, and you see a fish jump out of the water into the air, you won't catch any fish.

Pohnpeian Belief

Materials and Canoe Construction on Kapingamarangi

Like many low islanders, the people of Kapingamarangi must depend on the sea for transportation and subsistence. Consequently, canoe building is very important and requires time, care, and traditional skill.

On Kapingamarangi, only a few men are experts at constructing a canoe and these are older men. It is almost unknown for a young man to be a real expert at this skill.

If a man decides that he needs a canoe built, he should acquire some local food, and, perhaps, imported food if it is available and he can afford it. This food will be the only payment for those who actually build the canoe. He will then call upon one or two expert builders to work on his canoe and he will set a date for the work to start.

Building a canoe is a long process. First a large breadfruit tree must be found and cut down to be used as the hull of the canoe. It will be shaped and left to dry for about two or three months. Then the expert and his helpers will again work on the canoe. With six men working, it will take about one month to complete.

Both local and imported materials are used to build the canoe, although it can be made using only materials found on Kapingamarangi. Local materials include coconut husk ropes, two types of branches called *hedau* and *lagau haigo*, hibiscus to connect the outrigger to the canoe, and a long, thin piece from a coconut tree for the keel. Imported materials might be sails, line, and nails.

The larger canoes on Kapingamarangi are twenty feet in length. If the canoe is strong and goes beyond the reef it can hold as many as 200 tuna. I have personally seen a canoe with 130 tuna and it was not even sitting low in the water.

When the work is completed and the canoe is ready to be sailed, a ceremony will be held to celebrate the occasion. At this time a lot of good food will be served. The owner of the canoe will express his gratitude to the builders and will boast about the fine quality of the canoe.

There is another source of local materials used in making canoes that is not mentioned above, and this is the sea. Sometime drifting logs can be found that are large enough to use for building a canoe. However, they do not last as long as those built from the trunks of breadfruit trees. Also, when they are exposed to the sun for a long time, they tend to crack, causing leaks in the canoe.

Kapingamarangi has 33 islets, so canoes will always be important for the people. However, the younger generation does not seem to have much interest in the skill of canoe building and there is a danger that it might be forgotten in the future.

Big mouth!

Pohnpeian Proverb

Funeral Customs on Kapingamarangi

The people of Kapingamarangi have retained many of their cultural traditions since pre-Christian times, and this is especially true of death and burial ceremonies. A few changes have taken place, but generally the customs have survived the passing of time.

There are no cemeteries on the atoll and burial sites can be found scattered about the islets. The dead are often transported from one islet to another if there is a particular reason to do so. Upon the death of an 81-year-old woman, for instance, her body was transported to the place where her husband was buried and put in a grave. Long ago, houses were built over graves and presents were placed in them. These houses were then considered to be sacred and only certain people, such as the elderly, could stay in them. These were usually the burial sites for high chiefs, and they are still found on Kapingamarangi today.

When an important traditional chief dies, his body is wrapped in white pandanus mats. The people, to show their grief for the loss, weep and chant throughout the night and often cut off their hair. After being placed in a coffin, a flower garland is put on the chief's head. When the grave has been covered with earth, fine coral fragments are strewn about the area. If a woman dies in childbirth, this is a time of particular sorrow and special chants are said for her. When a child dies, his grandparents will hold the body all night while relatives and friends sing and give out wails of sorrow. Shortly before the burial, before the coffin is closed, it is customary for all people to walk around the coffin and say words of farewell or sprinkle the face with perfume.

A period of mourning follows the funeral and this is called *toruboo*, three nights, in the Kapingamarangi language. At this time, friends and relatives will gather at the home of the deceased. This is a serious time when comfort will be given to the family. On the first day, stories will be told that recount the virtues of the person who has died. On the following days, people will speak of the chiefs and heros who have passed away. At this time, there is no feast, nor is there any attempt to lighten sorrow with jokes or laughter. After toruboo, most of the friends will depart, although they can remain if they choose. However, family members will remain for a week or longer.

Unlike some other islands in Pohnpei State there is no large feast following a death and only light foods and beverages are served. On Kapingamarangi, a commemorative feast will be held on the first anniversary of the death. At this time, friends and relatives will again assemble, tell stories about the deceased, and attempt to comfort the family. Local foods will be served, especially eel, which is the most important food as feasts on the island.

The attention given to a funeral will vary, depending on who died. Chiefs, the elderly, and other respected people will receive much attention and a longer period of mourning. An infant who dies, however, will receive the least attention. One of the few changes that has taken place in recent times is in spiritualism. In pre-Christian times people prayed to the traditional gods. Today, people are influenced by the Protestant church on the island and pray to Jesus Christ.

If the sole of your foot is itching and you feel like scratching it with a knife, someone in your family will die.

Pohnpeian Belief

Federated States
of Micronesia

Kosrae State

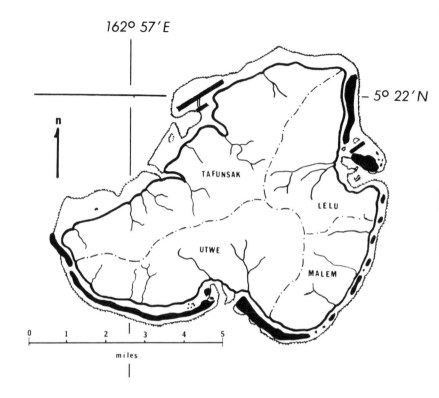

162° 57'E

5° 22'N

n

TAFUNSAK

LELU

UTWE

MALEM

0 1 2 3 4 5

miles

Kosrae

Land area: 42.00 square miles
Population: 5,522 in 577 households
Main Cultural Group: Eastern Carolinians
Main Language: Kosraean
Population Center: Lelu
Political: a state of the Federated States of Micronesia

If a couple fails to have a baby within a year of marriage, and adopts one, the wife will soon become pregnant.

Kosraean Belief

Childbirth on Kosrae

Kosrae is isolated from other islands of Micronesia. Our cultural practices combine the traditional with those brought by the missionaries in the last century.

Although there are no ceremonies before childbirth, certain customs are followed by many expectant mothers. Everything that she needs should be prepared before the delivery. According to custom, the woman should not go out at night. Otherwise, she will become very weak and will be sick when her child is born. Also, the woman is encouraged to be active, to exercise her body and to swim in salt-water. It is felt that if she does not do these things, she will have difficulty in her delivery. She is also restricted in the kinds of foods she may eat.

Responsibility for the pregnant woman is usually in the hands of her own mother. However, others who are familiar with delivering babies may be asked to assist. After the delivery and the severing of the umbilical cord, the husband will bury it and usually plant a coconut tree on top of it to mark the place. The new mother will be provided with food and also local medicine so she can gain strength. The baby will be kept warm by a local leaf that has been heated and placed on its body.

In Kosraean custom, the husband cannot stay with his wife after childbirth. He must stay in a different room or house for a number of months. The practical reason for this is so the mother or child will not contact diseases and become ill. The husband and other members of the family will provide her with food and limit the kinds that she eats. The foods given to her will have very little fat. Also, fish is considered to be the best food at this time.

The main celebration of childbirth on Kosrae takes place one year after the child has been born. Plans for the occasion will be made well in advance of the day and it is the husband's responsibility to organize it. On this day, very early in the morning, the mother will feed and wash her child and dress him in his finest clothes. The cooking for the feast will begin immediately and different foods such as breadfruit, taro, pigs, and chickens are prepared. Cooking takes place at the houses of both the husband's and wife's relatives. Although men do much of the cooking at this time, women and girls will assist. Also, every woman on this occasion will bring a gift for the baby.

When the cooking has been completed and all of the food is brought together, the father and child will select several men to distribute it. It is the mother's responsibility to keep track of the gifts and food. In the past, people would sing songs while presenting gifts, but this is no longer a practice on Kosrae.

There is little difference in the celebration even if the mother is not married. The only difference is that other male relatives of the mother would be responsible for the duties of the father. The actual celebration is the same for all children on Kosrae.

There are names given to children that are particular to the people of Kosrae and different names are given males and females. These names are traditional. Although they were given much more in the past, they are quite evident on the island today and the parents make this decision. Baby boys might be named Sru, Nena, Alik, Kilafwasru, Aliksru, Palik, Palikna, Alikna, Kun, Tolenna, Tolensa, and Tulenkun. Popular names for baby girls are Shra, Notwe, Tulpe, Shrue, Kenye, and Sepe, among others. Today, a combination of Christian and traditional names is given and anyone might name the child with the permission of the parents.

If a pregnant woman does not receive and eat the proper foods, her new baby will have an unwanted birthmark.

Kosraean Belief

Food and Eating Habits on Kosrae

Kosrae has been called the green island by some and the loveliest island in the Pacific by others. From the air or sea its lush vegetation presents a startling contrast to the blue ocean surrounding the island. An enormous amount of plant life exists on Kosrae. Although some were introduced during the Japanese and American administrations, most are native to the island.

Because of the rich soil and comparatively large size of the island, farming is quite common and every man should have farmland. Regardless of its size, he will have certain plants on his land. Some of these are breadfruit, bananas, wet and dry taro, and, most importantly, coconut trees. Coconuts are vital because they can serve as a food crop or a cash crop. The size of each holding is decreasing compared to landholding in the past. This is a result of increasing population and the splitting of an inheritance among a number of children.

Men do the farming on Kosrae and sometimes a group will work together as a team. They will come together and decide on which farm to begin with, whose will be next, and so forth. Most Kosraeans tend their farms individually, however. A farmer often takes his sons with him to help, and on Saturday an entire family might work. This is especially true if the father is a government employee and can only visit his land on weekends.

Farming usually takes place away from the home, but some crops are grown nearby in gardens. These might include sweet potatoes, cucumbers, watermelons, oranges, limes, and beans. Where oranges and limes are grown, only a few of these trees will be found because of the space necessary for the trees.

Because of farming responsibilities, it is difficult for a family to gather for meals and dinner is the only meal at which most families are together. On Sundays, however, people are not supposed to work and all three meals should be prepared the previous day. On Kosrae, there is no such thing as table manners as they are known in America. Also, people might eat only twice each day because it takes hours to prepare our main foods. People usually do not have breakfast unless they arise early enough in the morning to cook or they have something left over from the previous evening meal.

It is common on Kosrae that the father always has the first serving at meals so that he might have his choice of food. A special food might be served. If there is not enough for all, it would be unfair to the children if some had that food and some had to do without it. In this case, it would be best to leave it for the father and the mother. But most of the time, enough of all the foods is provided for the entire family. When the father is absent for some reason, the mother will assume his responsibilities.

In variety, Kosrae might have more different foods than any island in Micronesia. Fish are caught, animals are raised, and nature has been kind in providing an abundant diet of food from the land to Kosraeans.

Dropping a knife or a fork on the floor means that company is coming.
Kosraian Belief

The Importance of Land Ownership
on Kosrae

Land means life and is at the heart of every Kosraean. It is his most valuable possession and is something he would have trouble living without. To a Kosraean, land provides many things. Among these are a means of ranking a family or an individual in the village hierarchies and, of course, monetary value. By losing his land, a man gives away his life to be enslaved by others. Land also provides subsistence for the family and the household and goes hand in hand with life at all times.

All laws of land ownership on the island are associated with traditional customs and ownership is determined in several ways. Right of ownership by birth is the most common. In this way, land remains in a family generation after generation and it is sometimes owned collectively by a lineage or a clan. Giving of land to individuals within a clan must be spelled out clearly or disputes can arise between families and even among brothers. Trouble arises when a father divides his land unequally among his sons. The consequences of this can lead to serious disputes and the severing of ties between brothers and sisters. It can cause some to go so far as to denounce membership in a family. Many wise fathers, having seen difficulties in other families, refuse to divide their property among their children. Instead, they assure their children that since they were born into the same family, they have all acquired the same rights and privileges to use the land.

Another kind of land inheritance on Kosrae attempts to avoid disputes. In this type, the oldest child gets the most and the best lands. In this way, the oldest in the family, on behalf of the father, has the responsibility of dividing the land among the brothers and sisters. Since it is traditional in our culture to respect older people, many Kosraeans favor this method of distribution. The bad thing about it, however, is that the young usually never get much of the property.

200

Another kind of land distribution is where the parents favor some children over others. In this way, the younger children may be given a larger share of the property than the older sons. This, of course, is an insult to the older children, but they are helpless to protest. In land distribution, the parents' decision is absolute on Kosrae.

Possession of land can be a factor that makes children on the island want to please their parents. Some Kosraeans are convinced that if they show displeasure or disapproval to parents, it is like condemning oneself to a world without land.

Looking back when going away from one's home will bring bad luck.
Kosraean Belief

Changing Marriage Customs on Kosrae

There are many things that have not been written about marriage customs and ceremonies on Kosrae. Marriages are changing and these changes can be attributed to the introduction of new customs and culture on the island.

In our old customs, formal feasts were often held at weddings. A marriage was such an important affair that every member of the family had to take part and witness it. Both sets of parents of a couple had to approve the marriage. The families of the two lovers would meet and set the date for the event and a main topic of discussion at this time was whether the marriage should be formal or informal. A formal marriage had to be carefully planned and announced well in advance to all relatives and friends. It was the responsibility of the father of the young man to go around to all relatives and friends assigning duties for the event.

By tradition, formal marriage was more acceptable than informal marriage. Informal marriage is a practice by which the two lovers consummate their marriage without proper consultation of the church authorities. This was practiced at times, but the community looked down upon the couple as offenders in the society. Marriage was regarded as a very important occasion by

Kosraeans. It was an affair which required, by custom, that all relatives and friends contribute something for the occasion. The contribution, which would be called a gift, had to be prepared for a long period of time. There were certain ways in which gifts were valued. The longer it took to prepare a gift, the greater its value was considered to be. Time for preparation was a essential factor, much more than just the material value of the gift. On the wedding day, the families would gather all gifts and food in one place, but each family held on to their own gifts. Before the wedding ceremony took place, someone was chosen for each family to act as a spokesman. He would name everything brought by the family. In naming each item, he had to hold up the gift so that everyone in the gathering could see it. There was a lot of cheering, singing traditional songs, shouting, and dancing during the presentation of the gifts.

The wedding ceremony took place after the gathering of the food and other gifts for the feast. The wedding was usually done in the church, but in a case where a girl was pregnant before the wedding, the ceremony was not held in a church.

The contributions were distributed among both families, and the married couple received a greater share than others attending the wedding. The newly married couple was usually free to choose what family to live with. The choice was given to the couple, but they acknowledged that they were not independent; they could not live by themselves. No matter how old they were when they got married, they belonged to the groom's family.

There are many changes in our present day marriage customs in terms of time spent on preparation, the date to be selected, and the number of peole actually involved in preparing the food and contribution. However, what remains the same is that the marriage ceremony could not be held in the church if the bride is pregnant. Another case when the ceremony is not held in the church is when the bride has a child from somebody else.

If you drink from a coconut, and find no meat inside of the shell, it means that you will not marry until you are very old.

Kosraean Belief

How the Villages of Kosrae were Named

Kosrae is one of the largest islands in Micronesia. Although people can be found throughout the island today, there are still only four main villages, as there were in the past. A story is often told on Kosrae about how these four villages were first settled and how they were named.

It all began long ago with a mother, her three sons and her daughter, who stayed on a small portion of the island. As time passed, the mother grew to be very old and could no longer care for her children, so she called them together and told the children that it was time for her to let them off on their own and find homes on the island.

The oldest son wandered westward until he came to a place he wanted for his home on the western part of Kosrae. He named this place *Tafunsak*. The name comes from two Kosraean words: *tafu*, meaning half, and *sak*, which means woods or trees. He named his home Tafunsak because when he arrived there he found the place to be half covered with woods. Today, Tafunsak is the largest village on Kosrae because it was first settled by the oldest son.

The lovely daughter of the old woman settled the second village on Kosrae, and she called her home *Melem*, meaning moon. She chose this name because it was night time when she arrived there and the moon was shining very brightly. Melem looked so very beautiful under the moonlight. Because the daughter settled there long ago, young girls from this village are the most beautiful on the island even today.

The next oldest son wandered a great distance from his mother until he came to the far side of the island. He could go no further, so he decided to settle there. He wanted a name for his home, but he could not think of an appropriate one. Then he remembered that when he wandered there he had come to the back to find his home, so he named it *Utwe*, meaning from the rear.

The youngest son did not want to leave his mother and wander off to find a new home as his sister and brothers had done. Rather than leave his mother alone, he stayed with her until she died. When he was alone, he decided to name his home. As he looked around the whole area, he saw that it was completely surrounded by water. He decided to name it *Lelu*, meaning the inside of the lake.

The four villages of Kosrae still have their special qualities that can be traced back to the people who named them. Tafunsak is the largest because of the importance of an oldest son. From Melem come the most beautiful girls because it was settled by the lovely daughter of the old woman. Utwe is the village farthest south because the second son traveled the greatest distance to get there. And Lelu is very special. Even today it is the capital village of the island because it was the home of the mother and her last born son.

There are more pretty girls than one.

From a Kosraean Proverb

Extended Families in Kosrae

Kosrae has some differences from other islands in Micronesia. It is a high island and its people speak a language different from other areas in the Federated States of Micronesia. However, in the structure and function of the extended family, Kosraeans are very similar to all other groups of Micronesians.

In many parts of Kosrae the socially important group is not the simple family, but the larger group known as the extended family. The extended family consists of several generations held together through the male line, or the patrilineal line. Such a family many occupy a common residence, which may be a large section of land with separate houses for each of the smaller family groups, or it may have simple individual huts grouped together. The newly married couple will reside with one of their families and then they might settle permanently with the other. In some parts of the island, the people may choose where they will live, but rarely are they completely free from some form of supervision or control from one or the other of their families.

The traditional family system is strongly patrilineal and a household consists of the parents, their unmarried daughters, the sons, the son's wife, and the children. As the girls of the family married, each went to live with their husband's people and generally did only things for her own people as were allowed by her husband's people. If a woman was widowed, she continued to live with her husband's people who were still responsible for her and her children. This practice would continue until the woman remarries.

The older male of the family will be the head of the establishment when the father dies. A son remains subject to his father's wishes as long as the father lives and a woman is obedient to her mother-in-law. Most of the time, a father will have his wishes, since his son stays very loyal to him.

A family in the past might be housed in a single compound, or a very large house with as many as fifty persons. This included not only the persons mentioned above, but also the widowed mother of the oldest male or the widows and children of other male members of the family. There might be other dependent relatives from the mother's side also. Such households functioned as economic units, social units, and, to some extent, religious groups. They lived and worked together very cooperatively.

Although the extended family does not take over all of the functions of the single family group, it usually maintains an overall supervision of its members, and there are separate and clearly defined rights and duties involved. All extended family groups tend to place authority in the hands of the oldest members. In other words, the old people have the power to indicate their wishes, to say what they want to be done, and have authority over the younger members of the group. (Many years ago a young Micronesian teacher attempted to set up a community meeting house in a small section on Kosrae and received no response at all to the invitation he had sent out to every young man within the section. When a friend explained that it was the older people who would make the decision, the invitations were sent again, and this time to the elders in the community. The older people then came to the meeting, many of them accompanied by their sons, brothers and other young men. On Kosrae, the older people would decide what to do.)

A clan may be found in various sections of the island. Actually, clan members are descendants of a common ancestor and clanship is traced through the female line. In this respect, the children automatically belong to the clan of the mother. The extended family usually includes in its membership those who marry into the group, but such persons also generally retain membership in their own clan. The clan may be very large and may be scattered over the wide community. The related members who live far away may be unable to trace their specific relationships to one another even when they regard themselves as clan brothers or sisters. These clans usually have a clan name by which they are identified. The name is often of some animal and members of the clan might be identified as lizards, turtles, birds, or fresh water eel. Most clans serve to regulate marriage and one may be forbidden to marry a member of one's own clan.

Over the years there has been great change in Kosraean society. However, the extended family, with its duties, obligations, and rewards, remains much the same as it was in the past.

A child born on Sunday on Kosrae will have special good luck in his life.
Kosraean Belief

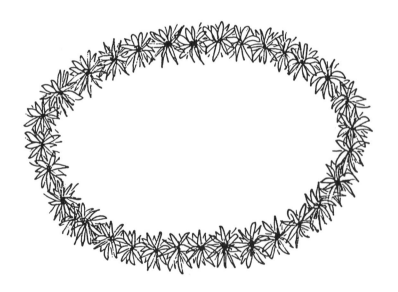

"*Mwaramwar*"

Fishing Methods on Kosrae

The island of Kosrae has significant differences from other islands in Micronesia. At five degrees, twenty minutes north latitude, it is the most southern of the high islands. Kosraeans also speak a language that is different from others in Micronesia. Although agriculture can sustain the islanders for food, fish is very important to the people.

Because of the clean and warm waters surrounding the island and the existence of a fringe reef, sea creatures can provide a good living. These differ in size, shape, habits, and their usefulness to man. The Kosraean names of some of the reef fish, which are eaten daily, are *mulap, aa, kupat, won, mesrik, kalisrik, scapsrap,* and *srinkap.* There are large fish beyond the reef and occasionally they come into the lagoon where the fringe reef is separated from the island. These are sometimes caught and are well known by their English names: tuna, barracuda, dolphin, and shark.

Kosraeans are skilled in several methods of fishing and different methods are required to catch different fish. With some methods men fish together and with others women do the fishing. Some methods are used by men together with women and even children.

Fishing beyond the coral reef is the responsibility of the men. Methods include trolling for tuna, catching flying fish at night with a net, and using a hook and line in water as deep as a hundred feet. Fishing under a full moon with a line for good sized redfish, just beyond the breakers, is also popular. All of these methods require particular skills, without which a fisherman can hardly be successful.

Fishing in the shallow waters of the lagoon with nets is done by women. They form a circle. As the fish inside of the circle try to swim away, the women catch them with hand nets.

Another method of fishing, *koamule,* is quite popular because many fish are caught, but it requires a good number of people. Men will gather coconut fronds and these are tied to either a long wire or locally made rope. It might be as long as a half mile in length. At night when the tide is high, men, women, and children pull the rope with fronds into the water. As the tide goes out, this acts as a fence to prevent fish from escaping. Then, when the water is low, everyone rushes inside to gather the fish which cannot escape because the water is too low. Children particularly love this kind of fishing.

The simplest kind of fishing is not necessarily the best and it is practiced by adults as well as children. On Kosrae there is a plant with a poisonous root. A number of these roots are collected and tied in bundles. Then these bundles are sunk in holes or crevices in the reef. As a result, the fish simply die from poisoning and float to the surface where they are gathered. The problem is in the waste. This method, of course, kills tiny fish as well as large ones that could be eaten.

Kosrae might have the best of everything as far as food is concerned in Micronesia. Its agriculture can easily support its population of 5,500 people. Skilled fishermen, using different methods of fishing, contribute to the diet of the people.

If you go fishing with coins in your pocket, you will catch no fish.
Kosraean Belief

Cooperation in House Construction
on Kosrae

Construction of a house on Kosrae is an event in which men, women, and children participate. It is a family affair in which all members help by assisting in what they can do best.

The person wishing to build a house must decide on the type to be built, the materials, the cost, and the kinds of labor he needs. He then will usually consult his neighbors and relatives about his plans and get their suggestions. He could ask them to contribute money or to prepare food for the day construction begins, or he might simply ask them to help with the building. It is required by custom that every member of the family is informed of the event and it would be an insult to one who was not notified so that he could help. Also, enough advance notice must be given so that each person has time to prepare for what he has been asked to do. When all planning had been done and materials collected, the relatives and friends will again be consulted to decide on the day that the actual construction will begin.

On the day the building starts, all who assist will come as early as possible. People will arrive with whatever has been decided upon. With wife and children, one man may arrive with a hammer and another with perhaps a saw or other tools. The wives and children will carry baskets of food they have been asked to prepare. The family head carpenter has responsibility at this time to see that enough tools are available and to send to borrow other tools if they are needed. While everyone is eating, talking and laughing, the carpenter and the owner of the house to be built would finalize plans and assign specific jobs. When the eating is completed, the work begins.

There is a division of labor in constructing a house, although this varies somewhat with the type of house being built. Women are supposed to prepare food but the older men are usually assigned to do the cooking. If the house is traditional style, the men and women will work together weaving thatch for the roof while the children haul gravel and sand. While the men take care of the *um*, or earth and stone oven, and boys kill and clean the pigs, women make soup and other dishes while children are bringing water and collecting firewood. The cooking will go on for several hours as the construction continues. Then, when the heavier part of the cooking is done, people relax and tell stories. The old men always seem to come up with the funniest jokes and tales that make the women and children laugh.

When time approaches for the meal, boys are sent to bring coconut fronds to be woven into plates and a special kind of basket for dinner. When the plates are filled with food, the men will stop working and everyone will eat, joke, exchange stories, and relax. After this, everyone will return to work. This pattern is followed until the construction of the house is completed.

The house that has been built can consist of all local materials, all imported materials, or a combination of both. Materials for a typical traditional house can easily be found on the island. There are mangrove trees for all purposes, palm fronds for thatch, and coconut fiber for securing the thatched roof. Imported building materials are expensive, but are available in the three main local stores on the island. With improved roads on Kosrae, access to more building sites has increased. Whether a house is traditional or modern style, the spirit of cooperation remains while building it.

Wounds to the body can be healed, but bitter words cause wounds that may not heal.

From a Kosraean Proverb

209

Present Funeral Practices on Kosrae

All dead on Kosrae are buried, although the ceremonies involved may vary according to the position of the deceased. Social status and popularity can win a lot of mourners, but, of course, the deceased did not consciously strive for this when he was living. It is just a last tribute that people pay to him.

All dead are usually not buried before a period of 24 hours has passed on Kosrae, and a person's age may determine the size of the funeral. The older people who die draw bigger crowds than infant deaths or suicides. The death that attracts the most mourners, however, is that of a pastor, another high clergyman, or of a chief magistrate.

When people die, the procedure for their funerals is the same throughout Kosrae. A church bell rings to announce the death to everyone. The ringing is different from all other announcements. The death toll is slow and singular. If the dead person was an adult, the bell will toll for about 20 minutes. For a child who has died, the bell will ring for about ten minutes.

The death must also be announced to other villages. A messenger relays the news quickly, regardless of the time of day or night that the death occurs. All deaths must be known through the entire island.

Meanwhile, the dead body is washed and clad in a white apparel especially prepared for the occasion. Then the body is placed in the middle of a room where the people can see it and mourn. While the women and the relatives mourn, the coffin is made and the grave is dug. During the night, choirs customarily sing religious songs until daybreak.

The feeding of the mourners is a big responsibility in a funeral. It worries the relatives and at the same time attracts people to the funeral. The foods gathered, donated, and prepared are of different varieties. If it is a big funeral, the foods might include pig, taro, breadfruit, sugarcane, coconuts, and rice, as well as coffee. A small funeral for an infant usually has less food. The family must take particular care to give everyone something to eat.

Before the body is buried, a service is conducted by the village pastor. If he is not available, a deacon takes charge. Following the service, the family and friends gather around the coffin to see the deceased for the last time. The body is then taken to the grave and the pastor gives the final burial service. During the last service, particular verses from the Bible are read and one or two hymns are sung. Then, the coffin is lowered into the ground and buried.

The funeral requires a big feast and the distribution of food is a very busy and worrisome task. Generally, the feast is divided up into ten different portions. The biggest one is given to the village from which most mourners come, and this is usually the same village where the death occurred. Four of the portions go to the other 4 villages. One goes to those who dug the grave and another one is shared by those who relayed the news to other villages. Still another is given to the men who made the coffin and another portion, which consists of the best foods, is given to the pastor. The final portion, of course, goes to the immediate family of the deceased. As soon as the food is distributed, people can leave. Customarily, however, the close relatives stay behind and keep the family company for as long as they wish. Some may remain for months, but others may leave sooner.

Normally it would cost the family quite a bit to feed such a large crowd, but a certain custom has been practiced for a long time to compensate for this. When people come to the funeral, they bring with them sacks of rice, sugar, coffee, biscuits, canned foods, pigs, and local foodstuffs mentioned earlier. These are added to what the immediate family can provide and about a third of the total food donation is set aside to be used later for two specific purposes. One is to feed those relatives who stay behind and the other is to take care of those who come to help make the tombstone and build a rock enclosure around the grave. Incidentally, there are no public cemeteries on Kosrae. All burial places are owned by individual families or clans.

A funeral is the saddest of occasions on Kosrae, however, the spirit of sharing, both In grief and in contributing food, always gives comfort to the bereaved family.

A *howling dog means that death is near.*

Kosraean Belief

Republic of the
Marshall Islands

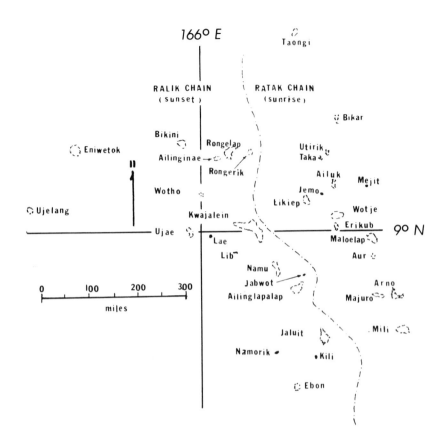

166° E

Taongi

RALIK CHAIN
(sunset)

RATAK CHAIN
(sunrise)

Bikar

Bikini

Eniwetok

Rongelap

Utirik
Taka

Ailinginae

Rongerik

Ailuk

Mejit

Wotho

Jemo

Likiep

Ujelang

Kwajalein

Wotje

Ujae

Erikub

90 N

Lae

Maloelap

Lib

Aur

Namu

0   100   200   300

Jabwot

Arno

miles

Ailinglapalap

Majuro

Jaluit

Mili

Namorik

Kili

Ebon

Marshall Islands

Land area: 69.84 square miles
Population: 31,043 in 3,829 households
Main Cultural Group: Marshallese
Main Language: Marshallese
Population Centers: Majuro and Kwajalein
Political: an independent republic with a
        Compact of Free Association with the U.S.A.

Fathers belong to us and to others, but mothers are ours forever.
        From a Marshallese Proverb

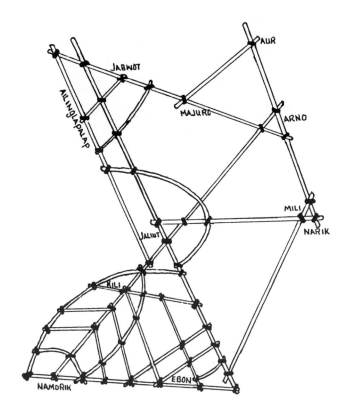

Marshallese Navigation Instruction Chart, "*Meto*"

If one dreams of floating alone on a raft at sea, a disaster will come to the household.

Marshallese Belief

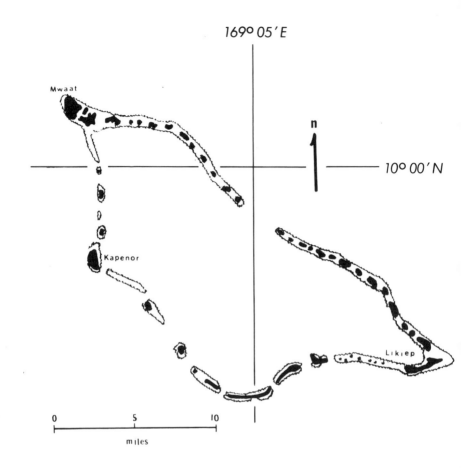

169° 05′ E

10° 00′ N

Mwaat

Kapenor

Likiep

0   5   10

miles

Likiep

Land area: 3.96 square miles
Population: 487 in 63 households
Main Cultural Group: Marshallese
Main Language: Marshallese
Population Center: Likiep Islet
Political: a municipality of the Republic
of the Marshall Islands

If a breadfruit leaf falls and lands with its smooth side upward, good luck will follow. If it lands with its rough side upward, one will have bad luck.

Marshallese Belief

Present Practices Before and After Childbirth
on Likiep

Childbirth in the Marshall Islands is considered to be a very important occasion. Consequently, on Likiep Atoll, activities take place both before and after a birth. To many superstitious minds, failure to follow certain procedures will cause illness or death to the mother and unborn child.

The pregnant woman's family and her inlaws will come together and ask their gods to protect the expectant mother and the unborn child. The purpose of this gathering is to pray in order to ward off evil spirits who are known to attack pregnant women. At this time, advice is given to the woman and plans are made for her care. All advice and plans must be carried out.

During pregnancy, a woman is required to rest and is not allowed to work at even relatively easy chores such as cooking and washing clothes. Her family and her husband's family will bring food and anything else that she desires. Pregnant women are rarely seen in public on Likiep as they must stay indoors as much as possible. However, a pregnant woman always has a relative staying with her. She particularly is not allowed out at night as some people, particularly the older ones, believe that evil spirits will attack her if she leaves her family.

At the time of the delivery, members of both the wife's and husband's families gather together outside of the house where the birth will take place. Enough food will be prepared for the group. As they wait, some will eat while others talk about various objects or subjects. It is forbidden, however, to talk about the birth because this might bring bad luck to the child or the mother. The purpose of this gathering is to show respect for the husband, the wife, and the expected child. The husband is the important person at this time as well as his father.

After the birth of the child, the same care for the woman is continued. This is the responsibility of the husband and his family. He will give certain responsibilities to various members. The younger sisters and the woman's mother are responsible for washing the clothes. The husband's mother also cares for the wife from the time of the birth until she regains her health and strength. The brothers of the husband should provide everything that the woman needs, such as coconuts, chickens, fish, and fruits. Until she is able to handle the home routine duties again, and assumes her responsibilties as a wife, everything, including caring for the baby and cooking, is taken care of for her.

A party might be held for the mother and baby as soon as they gain strength, especially if it is a first-born baby. However, the biggest celebration is held on the first anniversary of the child's birth. This is called *Kemem* in Marshallese. Members of both families of the couple prepare food for the occasion and many people attend, including important members of the community. The highly respected people who should not miss this celebration are the mayor, a priest, the owner of the village, the chief, and the husband's father. People will arrange themselves in a circle on the ground, and seated in the center will be the mother and child, the grandmother of the child, aunts, and cousins. Also, the respected guests will be seated along a table near the mat where the baby is sitting. At Kemem, people will sing songs as they present gifts to the mother and child.

There are two interesting aspects about our customs, besides those written above. One is that children are never orphaned, because the extended families insure that they will be cared for if anything happens to the parents. Also, whether the mother is married or unmarried, the ceremonies remain the same because of the importance of the child.

A pregnant woman should not go where there is fire or smoking, because smoke can kill the unborn baby.

Marshallese Belief

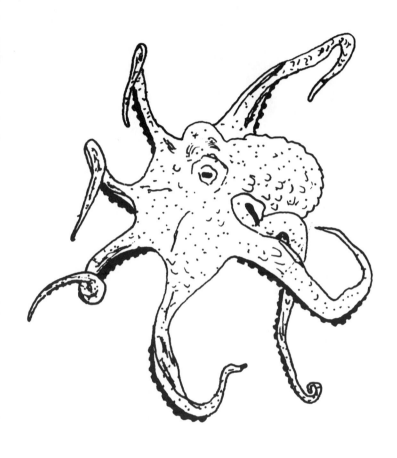

Octopus

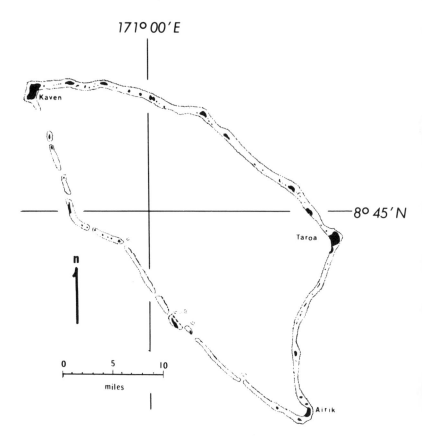

171° 00' E

Kaven

8° 45' N

Taroa

n

0   5   10

miles

Airik

Maloelap

Land area: 3.79 square miles
Population: 627 in 94 households
Main Cultural Group: Marshallese
Main Language: Marshallese
Population Center: Kaven
Political: a municipality of the Republic of the
    Marshall Islands

If one sleeps under a full moon, one will become moonstruck.

Marshallese Belief

Customs Before and After Marriage
on Maloelap

The Marshall Islands are spread over hundreds of thousands of square miles of the Pacific Ocean and are often separated from each other by vast distances. It is quite remarkable, then, that our customs regarding marriage are very much the same throughout the entire area. A couple desiring to marry on Maloelap in the west will have much the same cultural considerations as a couple desiring to marry elsewhere.

Before a couple marries on Maloelap, the marriage must be approved by the parents of both the man and the woman and especially by the older brother of the woman and sisters of the man. The older brother in a family is usually the one who has the most influence over the sisters according to the customs of the Marshall Islanders. At times the parents of the young woman may not wish her to marry, but if the marriage is approved by her older brother, she can marry without the consent of her parents. The older sisters in a family also have an influence over the affairs of a brother, and they must approve if the young man is to be married. If they agree, then he too can marry without parental approval. Although final approval for a marriage is in the hands of the older brothers and sisters, it is unusual if the parents disagree with them. A marryng couple usually has the consent of the eldest brother of the girl, the sisters of the young man as well as the consent of both sets of parents.

At the time that the young man and woman are ready to marry, the family of the man will have responsibility for the woman. They will provide for all of her needs, such as clothing and other necessities. The family of the girl will also have the same responsibility and they must provide for everything that the man needs for the wedding.

Attendance at the wedding ceremony is very important on Maloelap, as friends and relatives show their approval of the marriage by their presence. All of the relatives of the bride as well as those of the groom must attend. Since the atoll is less than four square miles in area, failure to attend because of not knowing about the marriage can be no excuse. If the relatives do not attend, they are showing by their behavior that they do not want either the boy or the girl to marry.

The wedding ceremony is followed by a feast which all the people on the islands are invited to attend. Many kinds of foods are prepared for this occasion by both the bride's and groom's family. The food is not exchanged between families but is prepared for all those who come to the celebration.

Many years ago the husband would live with his wife's family after the wedding. Today, however, it is customary for the married couple to reside with the family of the husband unless there are unusual circumstances that prevent this.

If a hermit crab is seen crawling in and then out of your house, you will soon move away.

Marshallese Belief

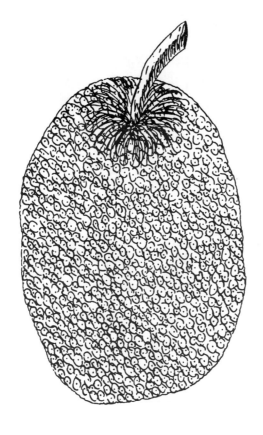

Breadfruit

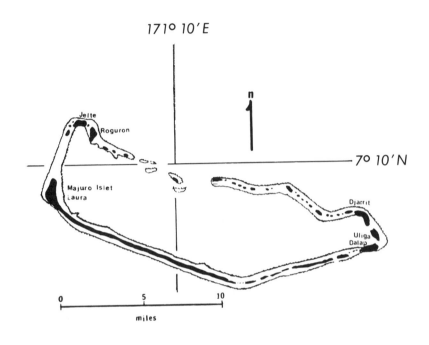

171° 10′E

n

7° 10′N

Jelte
Roguron

Majuro Islet
Laura

Djarrit

Uliga
Dalap

0   5   10

miles

Majuro

Land area: 3.54 square miles
Population: 11,893
Main Cultural Group: Marshallese
Main Lanugage: Marshallese
Population Center: Majuro and Laura Islets
Political: a municipality of the Republic of
          the Marshall Islands

If a man accidentally bites his tongue, he will have good luck in fishing, but three men fishing from the same boat will bring bad luck.

Marshallese Beliefs

How Reefs Were Formed on Majuro

A man named Letao on Majuro is famous in the Marshall Islands for his strength, but especially for his tricks and practical jokes that he played on others.

At one time Letao admired the canoe of a king and made a plan to trade for it. He decided to build an attractive, but useless, canoe and fool the king into thinking that the canoe of Letao was superior to that of the king.

A beautiful wood that is strong and shines called *kone* wood is unique because it will not float. Letao built his attractive canoe from this wood and shined and decorated it. Then he went to visit the king of Laura and offered to exchange canoes. The king said 'that he would come to look at the canoe on the following morning.

When the sun set, Letao pulled his canoe to the shoreline. At low tide he piled a number of large stones at a place offshore, and dragged his canoe on top of them. Thus, in the morning, when the king arrived, the canoe of Letao appeared to be floating on the surface of the lagoon.

The king was impressed with the appearance of Letao's canoe and did not even consider if it was seaworthy or not. So he gave up his proven craft in exchange for a canoe he had never sailed. Letao hurried away, leaving the king ashore admiring his new boat. He sailed quickly toward the pass leading to the open sea.

The king waded out into the lagoon and boarded his new craft, but when he tried to paddle away, his canoe would not move. He paddled harder, and suddenly his craft was pushed from the rocks, sank, and rested on the bottom of the lagoon.

The king, soaking wet and furious, yelled for his subjects to pursue and capture the tricky Letao. As canoes raced after Letao, he was laughing and singing. As his pursuers closed in, Letao kicked up sand and coral from the bottom of the lagoon. This caused the reefs to form that blocked their way. Still laughing and singing, Letao was last seen sailing into the sea beyond Majuro.

If one visits Majuro today, most people can tell stories of the popular Letao. And the reefs and sandbars in the lagoon are evidence that the story of Letao and the kone wood canoe is true.

Ghosts are approaching your village if birds are heard crying at night.
Marshallese Belief

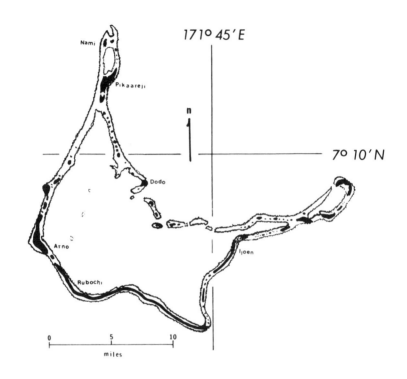

171° 45' E

7° 10' N

Nami

Pikaareji

n

Dodo

Arno

Ijoen

Rubochi

0   5   10

miles

Arno

Land area: 5.00 square miles
Population: 1,500 in 231 households
Main Cultural Group: Marshallese
Main Lanugage: Marshallese
Population Center: Arno Islet
Political: a municipality of the Republic of
          the Marshall Islands

If a butterfly comes into your house, you will soon have visitors, but if a hermit crab comes in, you will soon move to another place.

Marshallese Beliefs

Why Sharks Inhabit Lowakalle Reef
off of Arno

Before the foreigners came to the Marshall Islands there lived a man named Lowakalle on Arno Atoll. He is remembered as a very big and strong man and a fearful fighter.

One day Lowakalle left his people and went to live alone on an isolated islet called Ijoen. No one would visit him because he had warned all of the people to stay away. A long time passed and Lowakalle was nearly forgotten. In fact, his people did not even know if he was dead or alive. Those who passed Ijoen saw no trace of Lowakalle, but no one dared to go ashore.

Later on, the people of Arno began to complain about a stranger who visited each village, stealing their most precious possessions. No one knew how the stranger got to each village as there was no sign of footprints or a means of transportation. Then they remembered the mysterious Lowakalle, and began to suspect that it was he who was the thief. And they were right. Lowakalle would raid villages both day and night, and the way he would travel was by swimming. The people could not find a way of stopping him on the land as he was so very strong and powerful.

Then Lowakalle began his worst crimes. From his isolated island he would watch for cooking fires. He would then swim to the smoke, take all of the food, and kill anyone who got in his way. The people were terrified, but Lowakalle could not be stopped.

The situation was desperate, and so a meeting was called of the leaders of all of the villages. They had all suffered gravely and tried to figure a way of destroying Lowakalle. After much discussion, they decided that the only way to eliminate the monster, as they called him, was by deception. They would use Lowakalle's greed against him. After three weeks, everything was prepared. Many canoes set out for the best fishing ground of Arno. Ater arriving, they caught many fish. They then cut all of their catch into pieces and scattered the intestines about the area. This attracted many sharks.

Lowakalle, meanwhile, watched the fleet from his distant home. When he decided that many fish were being caught, he began to swim toward the area to steal them. Because he was so greedy, he swam very rapidly, right into the center of the sharks. They attacked Lowakalle, and he was killed and eaten.

227

The fishermen then returned home happily to spread the news that Lowakalle had been killed. The people of Arno felt safe again. To honor the event they named the reef where he was killed "Lowakalle," and it has this name to this day. Any visitor to the reef will find many sharks lurking about as a reminder of the story of the greedy Lowakalle.

Girls should not walk over boys' fishing equipment, or the fishermen will catch no fish.

Marshallese Belief

Attacking Shark

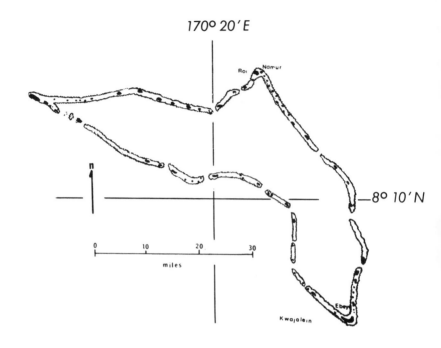

170° 20′ E

8° 10′ N

Roi Namur

Ebeye

Kwajalein

0　10　20　30
miles

Kwajalein

Land area: 6.63 square miles
Population: 6,629 in 643 households
Main Cultural Group: Marshallese
Main Lanugage: Marshallese
Population Centers: Roi/Namur, Kwajalein, Ebeye
Political: a municipality of the Republic of
　　the Marshall Islands

Be cruel, and you will have a short life. Be kind, and you will have everlasting life.

Marshallese Belief

Problems of Farming
in the Marshall Islands

Fish is the most important and accessible food in the Marshall Islands. However, foods grown on land are also a part of the diet. These are affected by the small land area of the atolls, quality of the soil, varying rainfall, and winds and typhoons.

The most popular foods grown are breadfruit, bananas, papaya, pandanas, and coconuts. Only a few other foods, such as sweet potatoes and pumpkins, grow on some islets. Canned foods and rice, of course, are imported.

There is twice the amount of rainfall in the southern part of the Marshall Islands as in the north. Even on individual atolls, however, it varies from year to year and this affects the size of the crops. Drought has always been a problem for the people of the Marshalls, especially in the north.

A number of modern farming methods have been tried in the past with little success and the people still practice traditional ways. Farming is not communal and is done by individuals on their own plots of land. Since farms are small, a family can usually take care of growing food on their land without additional help. Farming is done by both men and women and the family that cultivates the crop owns it.

Trading of produce takes place within the Marshalls. From December to April is the period of the strongest winds and heaviest rainfall, and this wind is used as motors for our canoes.

Plants have purposes other than to provide food. The coconut tree is used to provide materials for building our houses and the trunk of the breadfruit tree is used to make hulls for our canoes. Plants are also used to make local medicines and leaves are used to wrap food before it is cooked. They are also used as plates.

Since farming cannot provide much income in the Marshall Islands, fishing is far more important. The biggest sources of income, however, are from government employent and working for the Americans on Kwajalein.

Breaking a stone used for pounding pandanus will bring bad luck.
Marshallese Belief

Four Types of Fishing
on Kwajalein

Kwajalein Atoll contains the largest lagoon in the world, being more than 800 square miles in size. However, the land area of the atoll is little more than six square miles. This has caused fishing to be of great importance to the people. On the atoll, there are four main ways that fish are caught.

A common method of fishing is done with hooks and lines. In the past, the hooks were made from shells, but imported metal hooks have replaced these. The baits most commonly used are shellfish and sardines. Much hook and line fishing on Kwajalein is done at night. This type of fishing is done both from the ocean side, *latibben* or *liklok* in Marshallese, as well as *eolal* or *urok*, the lagoon side, often from canoes or boats.

Net fishing is also quite popular and this is done from the ocean side of the reef or in the lagoon during high tide. Nets manufactured in Japan and the United States have caused this type of fishing to increase.

A very traditional kind of fishing, passed on to us by our great grandfather, is done by using coconut fronds. This is called *alwelwe* in Marshallese and involves many men. Coconut fronds are first gathered together and are secured to a long length of rope. This is then brought to the reef at high tide and placed around an area of water in a circle. As the tide goes out, all of the fish within the circle are prevented from escaping by the fronds and are then speared or netted by the men. The rope used might be locally made from coconut husks or imported.

Another type of fishing requires skill in constructing a trap and is called *uh* locally. The trap is quite complicated to build and is made from the limbs of trees bent and tied together in the shape of a cylinder. The uh is built in such a way that there is an opening through which fish can enter. Once inside the uh, the fish are not able to leave the same way and are trapped until the fishermen arrive to collect them. Bait is placed in the uh to attract fish and a large stone keeps the uh under the water.

Fishing in the Marshall Islands has benefits other than providing food. Because of the necessity of fishing, the men of the Marshalls build very sturdy boats and are known as some of the best navigators in Micronesia.

Funeral Customs on Kwajalein

Possibly the most important traditional ceremonies on Kwajalein Atoll are those concerned with death and burial. This not only a family affair, but involves members of the entire clan of the person who has died.

It is our custom to immediately wash the body of a dead person using only special leaves called *konnat*. It is believed that these leaves will help to preserve the body and will slow decomposition in our hot climate. The washing of the corpse is done by close female relatives. The deceased is then laid out on locally woven mats and the body is decorated with flowers. This is done for all deaths regardless of the status of the person who dies. The only difference in funerals is that more people will attend the ceremonies for a chief than for a common person. The important procedures, however, are the same for all.

All of the friends and relatives of the dead person will come to the funeral bringing some gift as an offering. Some of these articles will be buried with the corpse and some will be given to members of the family. Money can even be buried with the corpse, as it is believed by some that the spirit of the deceased might travel to another place where it is needed. Since the Marshall Islands are dominantly Protestant by faith, a Protestant minister will usually conduct the funeral ceremony.

It is important that after one night, and no more, the corpse must be buried. As a result, burials will take place even during the worst weather. At the time of burial, each member of the deceased's family will follow the coffin in a procession to the grave site. Shortly before burial, prayers will be offered and important members of the community will give speeches. The coffin is then lowered into the grave and the chief will be the first person to pour a shovel full of earth into the grave. After this, the head of the dead person's clan will follow suit and then the rest of those attending will put earth into the grave.

Immediately after a burial is a very sad time for all families and so members of the clan will remain with the family. They might stay for as long as three or four weeks. This time is called *anak* in our language, and it is a very solemn occasion. No attempt at gaiety is made.

Seven nights after the death, the family will prepare food and call together all of the people who have not remained with the family. Then a feast will be held. It is believed that the seventh night following a death is the last time that the dead person will be with the family members.

All of our funeral customs must be strictly adhered to and all members of a dead person's clan must be immediately notified of the death. Failure to be told about a death can cause extremely bad feelings between clan members that might not be forgiven. Even if a clan member is on a distant islet of Kwajalein, word must be sent to him. A clan member's final resting place is with his own people.

Where there is kindness, there is life.

From a Marshallese Proverb

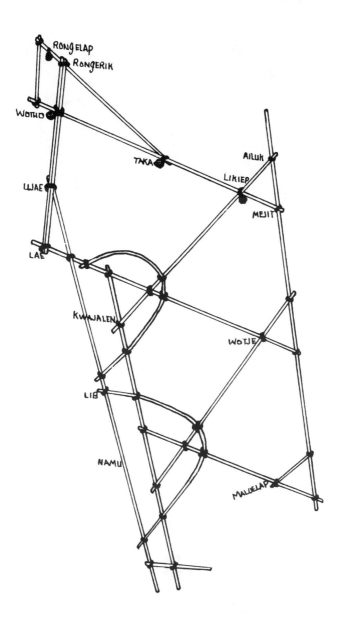

Marshallese Stick Navigation Chart, "*Meto*"

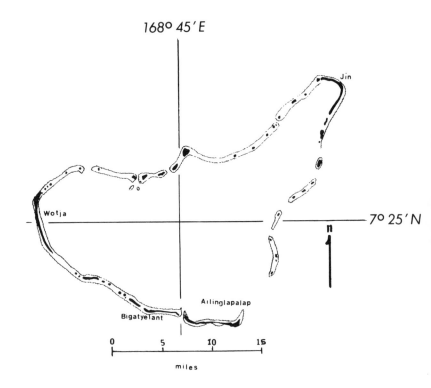

168° 45' E

Jin

Wotja

7° 25' N

Ailinglapalap

Bigatyelant

0   5   10   15

miles

Ailinglapalap

Land area: 5.67 square miles
Population: 1,400 in 156 households
Main Cultural Group: Marshallese
Main Lanugage: Marshallese
Population Center: Ailinglapalap islet
Political: a municipality of the Republic of
    the Marshall Islands

If a tree falls for no reason while the weather is calm, it means that a storm is on the way.

Marshallese Belief

Canoe Building on Ailinglapalap

It has been said that Marshallese men are experts at building canoes and boats. This is quite evident if you happen to observe old Marshallese men building a canoe on Ailinglapalap.

Canoes used in the past as well as today were made from the trunk of the breadfruit tree. No other tree was thought to be suitable by the builders. The local tools used, such as axes, planes, and saws, were made mostly from clam shells. Pandanus leaves were used to make a cord for measurements. Nowadays, however, stronger imported tools made from metal are used and more accurate measuring instruments have been devised. On Ailinglapalap, it may take only one expert to build a canoe. He may ask assistance if he desires, but most of the time the expert works alone until he completes the main body of the canoe. It usually takes months or can even take a whole year to build a large, seagoing, sailing canoe. A small canoe used for rowing takes a much shorter time to build, however.

After the hull of the canoe is finished, the expert chops down another tree, but this one is much smaller than the one used for the hull. The smaller tree is then shaped to make an outrigger. When it is finished, it is attached onto frames, called *kie* in Marshallese, and connected on the windward side of the canoe. A keel is always placed on the bottom of the craft to protect it from coral reefs.

Canoes are painted on Ailinglapalap. From the waterline upward they are usually painted white. Black paint is used from the waterline downward to the keel.

On the day that the canoe is completed, relatives will be asked by the builder to help carry the canoe to the beach. When it arrives at the shore, a dedication takes place. The local chief is always present and is seated at the best table covered with gifts. He will be presented with gifts after the dedication of the canoe. Local foods are prepared by the women and all friends and relatives are invited. A pastor always is present at this time. After he prays, the people eat. It is also customary to give the pastor gifts at the dedication. At the end of the ceremony, the canoe is carried to the sea to be tested. When it reaches the blue water, everyone claps their hands.

After the test, the canoe is carried up on the shore and this ends the ceremonies. The owner then thanks those who attended the occasion and goes home happily admiring his canoe.

Before going fishing, one must not walk near a cemetery, nor must one eat fish. Otherwise, no fish will be caught.

Marshallese Belief

Pacific Billfish

160° 35'E

Joluit

n

0   5   10
              miles

6° 00'N

Medyado

Emidj

Pinglap

Joluit

Jaluit

Land area: 4.38 square miles
Population: 1,485 in 202 households
Main Cultural Group: Marshallese
Main Lanugage: Marshallese
Population Center: Jaluit
Political: a municipality of the Republic of the
         the Marshall Islands

Seeing a whale swim close to shore means that a high chief will soon die.
Marshallese Belief

Death and Burial on Jaluit

On Jaluit Atoll, in the Marshall Islands, there are three important phases in a funeral, and the entire community is expected to participate in them. The islanders are expected to show respect to the dead before the burial, when the body is buried, and six days after the funeral. When a death occurs, the body is washed and covered with white cloth so that only the face is visible. This work is the responsibility of women. After it is decorated with sweet smelling flowers, the body is carried to a church where members of the community are expected to show respect by visiting the deceased. People will arrive from numerous islets of Jaluit, bringing gifts as a tribute to the dead. As the people arrive and depart leaving their presents, light refreshments are served by the family. Silence is maintained throughout the visits, except for the religious songs that are sung. After a period of 20 to 24 hours in the church, the body is placed in a coffin and carried to the graveyard.

The second important phase of the funeral takes place at the cemetery. Those who have returned home after visiting the deceased in the church are expected to come back for burial. When all are assembled and prayers have been completed, the members of the family of the dead will gather near the coffin to see or touch the body for the last time. As the men are looking on sadly and the women are crying, the coffin is nailed shut and lowered into the grave. The family members will take pieces of dirt and throw them on the coffin. Then, others in attendance will also throw dirt into the grave. Men will complete the burial by filling the grave to ground level. It is important that everyone has a chance to witness the burial and to participate in it.

The third important phase occurs on the sixth day after the burial. During these six days, the relatives tend to the grave by putting white stones on it. On the sixth day, people of the community return to find the grave clean, with beautiful flowers, and gifts such as towels, pieces of cloth, and woven handicraft around it. Prayers are again offered and then everyone is given a gift from the grave. One of the relatives comes to each person offering a last gift from the deceased. After the gifts have been distributed, an announcement of a big celebration is made. This is held either in the church or at the home of the family of the one who had died. On this occasion, speeches are made to encourage or strengthen the sad and lonely ones and songs are sung. Finally, a feast with lots of different foods is served by the family and other relatives.

If in your dreams you see any kind of boat, someone close to you is going to die.

Marshallese Belief

INDEX — SUBJECTS & ISLANDS

The Last area-wide census in Micronesia was taken in 1980. In 1993, the estimated population figures for the different entities were as follows: Republic of Belau, 16,000; Commonwealth of the Northern Mariana Islands (including temporary immigrant workers), 45,000; Republic of the Marshall Islands, 40,000; and the Federated States of Micronesia (including Yap, Chuuk, Pohnpei and Kosrae), 110,000. The greatest increase in population has taken place in the entity political centers while populations in the outlying atolls have remained relatively stable. When conditions become too crowded on the small atolls, some residents relocate and live with relatives in Koror, Colonia, Weno, Kolonia or Majuro. The political compacts between the Marshall Islands and the Federated States of Micronesia and the United States allow citizens of these areas free and unlimited access to American states and territories. Consequently, Guam, a U.S. territory, and the state of Hawaii have absorbed a considerable number of Micronesians in recent years. Overall, Micronesia has had a rather large population increase roughly estimated at three percent per year.

Some name changes have taken place since the last edition of *Micronesian Customs* appeared. Those most notable are Palau to *Belau* (although both are commonly used); Mokil to *Mwoakilloa*; Ngatik to *Sapwuahfik*; Truk to *Chuuk*; Moen to *Weno* The island names used in the individual stories are those originally written by the student authors.